CHARD-BRASIER

PE GORDON BENNETT 1904

h. Bellery Desfontaines

...SEMENTS GEORGES RICHARD

PARIS

EUGÈNE VERNEAU. PARIS

Art and the Automobile

Art and the Automobile

D. B. Tubbs

Grosset & Dunlap
A Filmways Company
Publishers · New York

A QUARTO BOOK

Copyright © 1978 by Quarto Limited
All rights reserved
ISBN 0-448-16425-6
Library of Congress Catalog Card Number: 78-69821
First Printing by Grosset & Dunlap, Inc. 1978 by
arrangement with Quarto Limited
Published simultaneously in Canada

This book was designed and produced by
Quarto Publishing Limited
13 New Burlington Street, London W1
Art Editor: Moira Clinch
Editor: Nicholas Fry
Editorial Assistant: Corinne Molesworth
Phototypeset in England by
Vantage Photosetting Company Limited, Southampton
Printed in Hong Kong by
Leefung-Asco Printers Limited

Frontispiece: *More serious artists are painting car subjects today than at any time in the past. This is true in France and in the United States, home of the Photo Realist school. Here the young English painter Ben Johnson avoids reflectionist clichés in this typically cool and architectural view of a* Glass Door Reflecting A Citroën.

Picture credits Anderson O'Day, London, 132b; Author's collection, 10 (photo Carl Henry), 11, 38b, 88t, 96tl, 124 (photos John Maltby); James O. Barron, endpapers, 6, 14, 17, 19c & b, 25t, 27, 28, 39, 41tr, bl & br, 42, 43, 47, 82t, 96b, 120t, 139tl & tr; Collection Geoffroi de Beauffort, Brussels, 15, 24b, 26tl & bl, 138, 140b, 141l; Dexter Brown, 117tr & br; Leo Castelli, N.Y., 122 (Coll. Chrysler Museum at Norfolk, Gift of Walter P. Chrysler Jr.), 123 (Private Collection); The Cleveland Museum of Art, Bequest of Lucia McCurdy McBride, in Memory of John Harris McBride II, 57t; Coys of Kensington Ltd., 68, 69, 73tl, 76t, 81b, 140tc; Terence Cuneo, 113, 115; Fiat Centro Storico, Turin, 73tr; Fischer Fine Art Limited: London, frontispiece, 133; Peter Helck, 112, 114; Nancy Hoffman Gallery, N.Y., 129, 130; Andrew Holmes, 119, 132t; Robert Indiana, 125; IPC Business Press Ltd., 82b, 90–91, 92t & l, 93r, 108t, 109l; Paul Kunkel, 33, 142; Robert Lamplough (photos Michael Fear), 13r, 32, 34–5, 36b, 37t, 55, 58, 59, 60, 73b, 94–5, 97l; Manx Technical Publications Ltd., 141b; Courtesy of Louis K. Meisel Gallery, N.Y., 131; Daimler-Benz AG, 116t;

Metropolitan Museum of Art, The Alfred Stieglitz Collection, 1949, 57b; Michelin Tyre Co., 20, 21t & c; Motor Sport, 64t, 108b, 136; Museo dell'Automobile Carlo Biscaretti di Ruffia, Turin, 110–11t, 111bl; Museum of Modern Art, N.Y., Mrs Simon Guggenheim Foundation, 121t; National Motor Museum, Beaulieu, 22b, 41tl, 48t, 49, 76b, 77t, 78t, 80r, 81t; Roy Nockolds, 105, 106–7; OK Harris Works of Art, N.Y., 127, 128; Collections de la Ville de Paris, 18tr; Hervé Poulain, 5, 8, 12, 13l, 18l, 21b, 23l & tr, 25c, 26tr, 29, 30–31, 36tl & tr, 37bl & br, 38t, 44t, 46, 50, 52l, 53, 54, 61, 62, 63, 64bl & br, 65, 66–7, 70, 72, 74, 80l, 87, 89, 92bc & br, 93, 96r, 97r, 98–9t, 98b, 100, 101, 103, 104, 134, 135, 139b; Pininfarina, 84; Rolls-Royce Motors Ltd., 140tl; Shell Mex and B.P. Ltd., 109c; Jasper Spencer Smith, 75, 77b, 78bl & br, 79, 83, 85, 137, 140tr & br; Tate Gallery, London, 52r; Michael Turner, 117bl; Waddington and Tooth Galleries Ltd., London, 126; Laurence Whistler, 141rc; Collection of Whitney Museum of American Art, 120b; Michael Wright, 116b.

Contents

Left: *A scraperboard drawing made for a Christmas card by Russell Brockbank, of the author in his car, a 1906 Gobron-Brillié 4–60 horsepower, happily discovered when Edwardian cars were cheap.*

Author's Note

I would like to thank the many friends who have opened my eyes to works which I might not otherwise have encountered, and who have so generously shared their knowledge. I must mention especially Peter Blair Richley who introduced me many years ago to Comte Geoffroi de Beauffort, whose collection of early works is quite outstanding, and who was kind enough in turn to introduce me to Maître Hervé Poulain, whose *L'Art et L'Automobile* (Les Clefs du Temps, Zoug, 1973) must remain the standard work. Not only has M. Poulain allowed us to reproduce many works illustrated in that volume, but with tremendous generosity he has made available many works which he has acquired since its publication. English colleagues, too, have been immensely patient and helpful, especially Peter Garnier and Brian Hatton, of IPC Business Press Ltd., while the author and publisher owe an immense debt to many other collectors who have made material available, notably James O. Barron, Robert Lamplough and Paul Kunkel in London, together with Peter Helck, of Millerton, N.Y., and David K. Bausch of Allentown, Pa.

Facing page: The strongest influence on motoring posters in the first few years was Art Nouveau, tinged in the case of Belgian artists with Symbolism, although naturalism was allowed to break through. This poster is by Privat Livemont (1861–1936), one of the great names in early poster design. He spent six years studying and teaching in Paris, before returning to his home town of Schaerbeek, where he won a poster competition. A virtuoso lithographer he always drew his designs directly onto the stone. This poster clearly depicts a de Dion, the Marquis de Dion being a member of the Salon committee.

7

Steam Coach to Horseless Carriage

Motoring prehistory in the 19th century

UNLIKE THE NUDE – in fact very unlike the nude – motor cars have only intermittently captured the imagination of the serious artist. Perhaps because there has never been a motoring Stubbs nor even a motoring Munnings the subject has enjoyed only incidental status, rather as some musicians tend to dismiss jazz and the Impressionists were rejected by French academic painters. It is amusing to remember that Claude Monet and Gottlieb Daimler were born within four years of one another, Daimler in 1836, and Monet in 1840, so that motor cars and modern art practically grew up together. Monet so far as is known never portrayed a car, but had he done so during his water-lily phase or during that wonderful season of London fogs and sunsets, he might well have done what Turner did for the railways in *Rain, Steam and Speed*. It must be confessed, though, that there was little speed about Gottlieb Daimler's original creations, and the motor car only gathered pace at the hands of his engineer, Maybach, and of the experimental department at Panhard's as racing came into its own and, simultaneously, the depiction of speed developed into a minor art.

The relative lack of motor car paintings does strike one at first as odd. There have always been artists interested in mechanism for its own sake and they have never lacked machine-loving patrons.

Leonardo da Vinci delighted in machinery; he even invented and drew the earliest wheel-lock pistol, and modern experimenters have shown that it would have worked; which is more than can be said for Hans Burgkmaier's splendid hand-powered military vehicle in *The Triumph of the Emperor Maximilian*. In short there is a very strong tradition of technical art from the earliest times: church brasses

Facing page: *Emile Guillemin (1848–1909) made this remarkably prophetic lithograph about 1903. The road racing cars, low-built for their day, make an interesting contrast with the sporting turnout shown in C. B. Newhouse's* Cocking Cart Going to the Moors *(below).*

9

The world's first wave of mechanical road transport came in the 1830s, when a number of inventors designed and operated steam coaches in England. One of the most advanced of these was a project by W. H. James shown in this drawing taken from the 1833 Patent application. Prophetic features included a forced-draught boiler, and the three-speed transmission by means of chains and dog-clutches which anticipated G. N. and Frazer Nash sports cars by 75 years. The gas head-lamp will also be noted.

enable us to follow the development of armour almost year by year; thanks to Renaissance paintings we know when watches were first worn and exactly what they looked like, and the details of blued-steel and gold damascened plate armour obviously appealed as greatly to such artists as Hilliard, Mytens, van Dyck as they did to those who were responsible for commissioning them to be made.

Why should painters feel at sea with the car? Marine artists have always known which rope did what, whether one thinks of Ancient Egyptian barges, the Bayeux Tapestry in its less intimately domestic moments, or British and Dutch sea-pieces of the 17th, 18th and 19th centuries. Nor is it simply the overall picture: James Tissot,

judging from the ships' furniture in the background of his steamer paintings in which mahogany and brass contrast so delightfully with the silks and satins of his ladies, would have delighted in the lamps, horns and levers of a *fin-de-siècle* car. That spidery turnout itself would have attracted Constantin Guys, perhaps the most delicate painter of carriage scenes who ever lived; but when Guys died in 1892 he was the same age as the century and motor cars had only just begun to appear. A pity, for his delicacy of touch would have been perfect for the frail lines of a rear-engined Peugeot or Benz.

Carriage art deserves more than a passing mention, since it was largely the coachbuilder and his customers who were

with the horses' heads, for the inside of the cart was tall enough to carry gun-dogs or fighting cocks going to a main, and the horses were driven tandem – one behind the other. Danger has always been the essence of sport.

Danger there was in plenty during the pre-history of the car. During the hey-day of coaching, that is to say between about 1820 and 1835 when J. L. McAdam used hard stone broken small to build roads 'smooth, solid, and so flat as that a carriage may stand upright', and during the railway boom of the 1840s which killed road transport for nearly sixty years, sundry 'noblemen, gentlemen, and engineers' sought to make the best of two worlds by running steam coaches upon the roads. Many were of advanced design and some, according to evidence before a Parliamentary Committee, travelled at speeds up to 35 mph. These form a fine zoo of prehistoric monsters in the history of motoring art. Naturally they attracted caricaturists, for although some were not unlike stage coaches to look at, others (probably the ones which never got beyond the financial-prospectus stage) could have rolled, hissing and steaming, from a production of *Cinderella*. Some were quite practical, operating bus services in London for months at a time. Others, if one may believe the cartoonists, were ungainly gingerbread monsters like an explosive Lord Mayor's coach, flying asunder and peopling the air richly with severed arms and legs. The best of them were built by Hill and his disquietingly named partner Burstall; Sir Charles Dance; Walter Hancock and Goldsworthy Gurney (who was later knighted for something quite different), and the litigious Captain Macerone. One of the most ingenious was that of W. H. James, who invented a three-speed gearbox using chains, sprockets and dog-clutches of precisely the sort used on G. N. and Frazer Nash sports cars from 1910 until 1937. The road steamers have their place here because numerous artists wreaked their will, factual, imaginary, comical or macabre upon them, including J. Doyle, Henry Alken, Luke Herbert and George Cruikshank (1792–1878).

Caption-writers were given their head: the Doyle is called 'A Sketch of Mr. Gurney's New Steam Carriage as it appeared at Hounslow on the 12th of August with a Barouche attached containing the Duke of Wellington and other persons of Distinction'.

The Gurney steam coach was immortalized in various ways. Perhaps it

Contemporary with its subject, this 14-inch glass toddy-rummer for hot punch carries a copper-wheel engraving of Goldsworthy Gurney's 1827 steam coach. The drawing is simplified from a well-known print, which may be seen reproduced in the Badminton Library volume on Motoring, published in 1901.

to dictate what motor cars looked like, and therefore, almost as important from our own point of view, what clothes people would be wearing in them. Many of the tricks employed so successfully by motoring artists were already known to coaching and carriage artists like George Garrad, James Pollard, John E. Ferneley, Henry Alken, Sr., J. F. Herring, Sr., Charles Cooper Henderson and the author's favourite, C. B. Newhouse (*fl.* 1830–1845), whose *Cocking Cart, Going to the Moors* shows what must have been one of the most exciting vehicles of all time, Formula One cars not excepted. The owner drove this two-wheeled turnout standing up, with a passenger beside him and a groom perched behind. His feet were on a level

The French car industry grew directly out of the cycling boom which gripped Paris during the 1880s and 1890s when all classes joined the Sunday parade in the Bois de Boulogne. In this lithograph, entitled Retour du Bois le dimanche, *one of the earliest motoring documents, the Swiss illustrator Théophile Steinlen (1869–1923) shows three big steamers, most probably by De Dion, and a light* voiturette.

was a satisfied passenger who purchased the 14-inch glass toddy-rummer on page 11. The spirited copper-wheel engraving was based on a popular print, the original of which shows the coach passing a country inn. This print was published in several languages and it may have been the Italian version which brought to England in 1835 an engineer in the Sardinian army named Virginio Bordino. On returning to Turin Bordino built five effective steamers, number three of which can be seen in the car museum in Turin, founded by the late Conte Carlo Biscaretti di Ruffia. Motoring history owes a great debt to that charming Count, for not only did he rescue the Bordino coach, but he also amassed a large collection of other early vehicles (being virtually the only car collector in Italy before the Second World War) and arranged for the building of the museum.

In Britain a few lonely country gentlemen experimented with light steam carriages during the 1860s and 1870s and can therefore be called the first real motorists; but they did not venture far from home. Amédée Bollée at Le Mans in 1873 picked up where Gurney and Bordino had left off, making splendid trips to Paris in his independently sprung coach

l'Obéissante, now in the Musée de la Voiture at Compiègne. A charming drawing of it, though not contemporary of course, was made by that great French illustrator Georges Hamel, known as Geo Ham. Steam coaches had their day. Then in the 1880s Benz and Daimler in Germany substituted petrol for coal as a way of making cars run, and the Comte Albert de Dion, aristocrat, gambler, duellist and *bon vivant* with a taste for machinery, put new life into steamers, first with tiny steam tricycles, then with coke-fired tractors capable of pulling a carriage or running under their own steam.

Anything the Comte did was news. It is almost certainly some of his steamers that sinewy draughtsman Théophile Steinlen captured in his lithograph *Retour du Bois, le dimanche*, which, being dated 1889, must be one of the very first illustrations, apart from photographs, made of an automobile on the road.

Some pretty postcards based on watercolours bearing the same date may also be found, signed, apparently, Henri Boutet: pretty girls, the infallible approach.

During the early 1890s motoring as such began to get off the ground. In Germany the primitive Benz proved an ideal vehicle for moving around fashionable spas like Baden Baden and Wiesbaden, although little use outside town. The real place for motoring was France.

In 1893 a letter signed 'Jean Sans Terre' appeared in the Paris paper *Le Petit Journal* suggesting a competition for *voitures sans chevaux*. The writer was Pierre Giffard, editor of the paper, and the idea soon gained support. In 1894 therefore what we should call a rally was held from Paris to Rouen. The public, judging by a photograph of competitors passing through Mantes, found it a monumental yawn; but 'the new locomotion' had in fact got off to a flying start. A committee was formed to run a proper race the following year over the great Roman and Napoleonic *route nationale* from Paris to Bordeaux and back, a distance of 732 miles. This event, the world's first long-distance road race, was won by Emile Levassor, the tough and brilliant engineer partner in the firm of Panhard et Levassor. He made such good time on the outward journey that his co-driver was not at Bordeaux to relieve him, and he therefore turned straight round and drove single-handed back to Paris, making the round trip in a few minutes over forty-eight hours – an astonishing drive on solid tyres considering the state of the roads and the primitive nature of his machinery. Levassor became a national hero when he crossed the finishing line at the Porte Maillot, and the French motor industry was launched. Panhard, Peugeot, De Dion and the rest found their order-books full and were able to build up a substantial clientèle among fashionable Parisians.

They were able to do this thanks to an accident of geography known as the Bois de Boulogne. The Bois is a large tract of park and woodland criss-crossed with roads lying to the west of Paris and forming a natural barrier between the fashionable areas of the capital and industrial suburbs such as Levallois-Perret, Courbevoie and Boulogne-Billancourt. Here, during the 1890s, early morning lessons in cycle-riding had been taken in reasonable privacy and here later in the decade came learners with their first horseless carriage or, more daring still, motor-powered tricycle. As the Bois lay within a few minutes' carriage drive of Neuilly, Passy or the Faubourg St. Honoré, ladies, gentlemen and demi-mondaines could keep rendezvous with an instructor and, after the lesson, be driven home to breakfast. Later, when proficient, they could join the fashionable parade undismayed by thoughts of breakdown. The manufacturer's establishment was within call across the Bois and he would supply an instructor/mechanic.

It would have been here that Dr. Gabriel Tapié de Celeyran, Henri de Toulouse-Lautrec's cousin and fellow reveller learned to drive. Lautrec's portrait, or caricature, of Tapié is probably the first motoring portrait of all and sums up the earliest days of motoring. Tapié sits grasping the tiller of his Panhard, anonymous in mask

Below, left: *Perhaps the first motoring portrait, this lithograph by Henri de Toulouse-Lautrec (1864–1901) shows the artist's cousin and fellow reveller, Dr. Gabriel Tapié de Celeyran wearing the accepted garb of the period – chauffeur's cap, goggles and leather mask, and peau de bique fur motoring coat.* Below, right: *This charcoal drawing made as a historical exercise by the French artist Georges Hamel (born 1900) shows one of the world's very first private cars, 'La Mancelle', built by Amedée Bollée the steam coach pioneer, at Le Mans in 1878. Bodied as a victoria, it was remarkable technically in having shaft drive to a crown and bevel rear axle. Note the three-man crew – coachman and footman on the box and chauffeur (stoker) behind.*

and goggles, swathed in a shaggy motoring coat.

Graham Sutherland once remarked that Lautrec, had he lived, would have been the greatest motoring artist of all time; and when one looks at the exquisite dog-carts, shooting-brakes and gigs drawn before his descent on Paris, there is no doubt that he was right. Lautrec caught the movement, the lines of the coachwork, the glint of light on the wheels just as Constantin Guys had done, and he set the whole carriage in motion. Unfortunately this most evocative of artists died in 1901 at the age of thirty-seven, but we can be sure that he would have struck sparks from a subject which so delightfully blended two of his principal interests, namely *le sport* and *le high-life*. We know he was at least mildly interested in things technical; he used to frequent the Vélodrome Buffalo in Paris with his friend 'L.B. Spoke' – an anglophile named Bouglé, whose firm, Cycles Michaël was the French agent for Simpson chains, for which Lautrec drew several posters. The chains and sprockets in these show that he was less at home with cycling than with human or equine anatomy, but the movement and the interest are there and there can be no doubt that if Lautrec had enjoyed a few more years of life, cars with him would have become both a necessity and an enthusiasm. His friends Alexandre, Thadée and Mysia Natanson would have seen to that, for during his last five years as an invalid motoring, launched by the cycling boom of the early 1890s, had been gaining converts every day. He would infallibly have discussed the subject with his friends, and with fellow poster-artists such as Jules Chéret, Eugène Grasset, Steinlen and PAL, alias Jean de Paléologue, together with the poster artist and caricaturist Jules Forain, a very keen driver, himself caricatured by SEM in the Paris-Berlin race of 1901.

At *La Revue Blanche*, the literary magazine which the Natansons founded in 1891, Lautrec would have been in contact with motoring from the very first, for among his fellow contributors were such enthusiasts as Tristan Bernard, Guillaume Apollinaire, Max Jacob, the novelist Octave Mirbeau and Pierre Bonnard, who later collaborated with him. An eclectic, brilliant assembly.

Motoring art at this time mainly took the form of posters, usually allegorical in treatment, and caricature, for early motorists and their adventures were fair game for the funny papers. There was one artist, however, who took the subject more seriously.

This was Albert Robida, who was born at Compiègne in 1848 and died in Paris in 1926. Robida's output was tremendous. He edited an illustrated magazine called *La Caricature*, drew for other papers as well, and illustrated more than a hundred books. He was also a writer of science fiction rather on the lines of Jules Verne, and scored a great hit in 1882 with his prohetic novel '*The Twentieth Century*' which he illustrated himself and followed with another, even better, *La Vie Electrique*. Robida had a sharp eye for fashion, and knew how to put movement into his cyclists and cars. When therefore the motoring enthusiast Pierre Giffard wrote his provocative book *La Fin du Cheval* in 1899 he naturally turned to Robida for the illustrations.

It was because of their role as book illustrations that the Robida drawings were able to treat their themes figuratively. The same applied to what were called the minor arts – the making of decorated watch cases, inkstands, pen-knives and the like on automobile themes. But once he moved outside what may rudely be called the 'souvenir bracket' an artist was expected to become classical or mythological, even on objects such as competition medals. There were signs of change, however, and that change was due indirectly to Albert Robida's patron, Pierre Giffard.

The first motor show was held in Paris, organized by the committee which had been responsible for the Paris–Bordeaux–Paris of 1895. The poster opposite is signed E. Clouet, the car probably taken from a photograph. Early motoring art was mainly allegorical or humorous, but commercial artists allowed themselves a naturalistic approach in posters and objects like the silver watch shown below. The original water colour (bottom) was made by Albert Robida as a frontispiece to La Fin du Cheval *by his friend Pierre Giffard, motoring enthusiast and editor of* Le Petit Journal.

Racing Monsters

The early motor races, 1895-1905

WHEN EMILE LEVASSOR, hero of the Paris-Bordeaux-Paris race of 1895, died as the result of an accident (he hit a dog and his car overturned during the Paris-Marseilles-Paris race of the following year), the job of providing a monument was given to one of the most eminent sculptors in France, Aimée-Jules Dalou (1838–1902). Dalou was a good choice because like Courbet, to whose paintings his sculpture had been compared, he had strong notions of reality and was one of the founders of the Salon des Indépendants. A subscription was opened by Pierre Giffard, editor of the *Petit Journal*, one of the great pro-motoring influences of the time, with the Marquis de Dion as chairman. Nearly £1,500 was raised – not a bad sum in those days – and Dalou accepted the commission with some reluctance. The task, he noted in his diary, was to make 'a monument to a victim of automobilism' and he added, 'the fee is poor and the subject not very inviting'. Then he cheered up. It might after all be fun, a challenge, and a chance to flout orthodoxy. On May 14th 1898 he wrote, 'The job is to make a monument/advertisement for the motor car. An advance on pictorial posters; this one will be marble; it won't wash away in the rain.'

Dalou realized that he was truly breaking fresh ground. Machinery was not then considered a fit subject for art. 'Industry, no!' Ingres had cried thirty years before, 'we want nothing whatever to do with it!' In Dalou's notebooks are no fewer than thirteen sketches, starting conventionally with the mythical goddesses and moving steadily towards a naturalistic high relief of Levassor in his actual car, passing through an imaginary triumphal arch at the Porte Maillot. First he made a plaster model of a rather stylized motor car and crowd, then a more naturalistic one. This final version, cast in bronze by the lost-wax process, was enthusiastically received by the committee, and Dalou then elaborated, to a larger scale, the details of the driver, crowds and car, correcting certain items of equipment on the Panhard such as the lamps. Evidently he had come to have a serious regard for his 'marble poster', the first work connected with cars to be commissioned from an artist of renown. It is fascinating to watch, by way of Dalou's sketchbooks and models, his interest in technical details. At first he evidently saw it as yet another monument, then, abandoning allegory, he concentrated on the architectural setting, almost to the exclusion of the subject-matter. Finally, he homed in on the automobile.

After Dalou's death completion of the monument was entrusted to his pupil, Camille Lefèvre, who translated the plaster into a marble carving in high relief. The delicacy of Dalou's arch disappeared somewhere along the line, giving place to

The death of Emile Levassor (right) in 1896 deprived the early motoring world of one of its great heroes, and a monument was commissioned from one of France's leading sculptors, Aimée-Jules Dalou.

Exiled in England after the Commune, Aimée-Jules Dalou (1838–1902) became, with Rodin, one of the most famous sculptors in France. Dismissive at first of the Levassor monument commission as a 'poster in marble', he rapidly grew keen, and produced a series of increasingly naturalistic maquettes, including that shown above right. Following Dalou's death a final version was carved in marble by his pupil Camille Lefèvre, and unveiled in 1911. The monument (above) stands at the Porte Maillot in Paris.

the heavy Edwardian baroque that was only to be expected as King Edward's reign advanced. The monument was eventually unveiled in 1907, an astonishing example of technical realism in an age which still could not dissociate motorcars from the Goddess of Speed. Amateurs of automobile sculpture should make a pilgrimage to the Porte Maillot, with a side trip to the Place St. Ferdinand to see a monument erected in 1911 to the steam-car pioneer and ex-holder of the Land Speed Record, Léon Serpollet. Executed by a sculptor named Jean Boucher (1870–1939), this is a more romantic, less realistic piece.

Levassor in his monument is receiving a hero's welcome, and perhaps for that reason wears a bowler hat rather than conventional motoring attire. Usually in those days the 'autocarist' was a figure of fun, rather like the 'cads on castors' as early cyclists had been called. Open-air motoring without bonnet scuttle or windscreen

was a cold business, for which French drivers dressed in bear-skin or goat-skin *(peau de bique)* coats, topped with face-mask and goggles, to the delight of cartoonists like Weiluc. Perhaps steamers provided central heating, for in the *Retour du Bois* already mentioned Théophile Steinlen (1869–1923) makes his driver perfectly matter-of-fact as he forges through crowds which would make a modern London-to-Brighton Run competitor feel perfectly and uneasily at home. Steinlen, who came to Paris from Lausanne, quickly made a name as a poster artist, and must have been one of the first to receive commissions from the motor industry. Around 1895–1896, at the height of the cycling and motor tricycling boom, he drew posters for Motocycles Comiot showing a girl on one of the dashing new motor tricycles in the midst of a flock of geese. Those geese might be anywhere, but the peasants in the background take one almost by surprise. That rural setting, so adventurously removed from the Bois, should be English rather than French.

The approach to motoring – and therefore to motoring art – was almost startlingly different in the two countries. While motor car users in France, like fashionable life generally, were based largely on Paris, the English pioneers were scattered throughout the length and breadth of the country, while the industry, such as it was, was based on the Midlands, where bicycles were made. English motoring was an odd blend of cycle-shed and country house. Men like Stocks, Charles Jarrott and S. F. Edge were racing cyclists before they discovered engines; open-air sportsmen, eccentric in preferring 'stink wagons' to horseflesh, but really little different from their friends who spent their days on the moors, on the river or on horseback. England in those days was a country of fresh-air fiends. Cycling improved the health and developed the calf-muscles. It was uncomfortable enough to be godly – a sort of ambulant cold bath – and motoring when first imported was looked upon not only as a mechanical adventure but as a form of cycling for invalids.

'I have known instances of ladies suffering from defective nerve power who have derived great benefit from the invigorating and refreshing effect of meeting a current of air caused by driving in an automobile. Veils of varying thickness, according to the temperature, should, of course, be worn by ladies, but much of the benefit to nervous patients is caused by the air blowing on the face', wrote a well-known Harley Street doctor (English, of course) in the Badminton Library's *Motoring* in 1900.

By the mid 1890s certain Parisiennes, by no means suffering from defective nerve-power, were already to be seen darting about the Bois clad in Mrs. Amelia Bloomer's brainwave on motor tricycles powered by the Comte de Dion's new high-speed petrol engines, or ensconced in that elegant little open car called a *duc*, which looked just like a pony phaeton unharnessed. At this time, wrote Maurice Farman in his *Manuel du Chauffeur-Conducteur*, Messrs. Panhards did their best to make their cars resemble carriages, but, he added, although these cars were quite smart they 'looked as though something was lacking, and that something was a horse'. Very soon long bonnets would arrive to redress the balance; but in the meantime a doorless *duc* or Park phaeton with no horse to spoil the view made a perfect setting for aristocrats and demi-

mondaines alike – and the latter especially made the most of their motors. Liane de Pougy, from the Folies Bergère, had a Krieger electric, and her rival, Caroline, known as La Belle Otéro, had a De Dion with a black motor boy.

English car owners, whether country squire, professional man or mechanic, were isolated from their fellow sufferers by miles of rough, hostile, police-infested road, learning, driving, pushing, being towed, having accidents and mixing with horsey neighbours, to the incessant delight of *Punch*. Comic artists made the most of this, on both sides of the Channel: Weiluc has already been mentioned, and in addition there were René Bull (one of the earliest, 1894), Stuart Travis, Lance Thackeray, Harry Elliot and, a little later, G. E. Studdy, of 'Bonzo' dog fame.

English motorists prided themselves on their restraint. Dr. Fred Lanchester and his brothers sold cars that had virtually no brightwork, and which thanks to the perfectly balanced engine were far quieter

By 1896 the English black-and-white artist René Bull (top) had hit on the sure-fire formula: man+girl+status symbol, which car advertisers have been using ever since. The posters for Hurtu and De Dion Bouton date from the first years of the new century.

The Michelin Men

The brothers André and Edouard Michelin pioneered pneumatic tyres for cars by themselves using them in the Paris–Bordeaux–Paris race of 1895. They also encouraged artists of all kinds. The London building of the Michelin Tyre Company on the corner of Fulham Road and Sloane Avenue (left, top and bottom), *like the Paris headquarters in the Boulevard Pereire, was the work of a staff architect, François Espinasse. It is one of the purest Art Nouveau buildings extant, and dates from 1910. The 'Michelin man', alias Bibendum, who drank obstacles, was created by the artist O'Galop, whose real name was Maurice Rossillon* (centre, top). *Figure and slogan* Bibendum *('Let us drink . . .') are still used today. The mosaic* (centre, bottom) *is in the London Michelin building, which is decorated inside and out with coloured tiles which form a contemporary picture gallery of the company's racing successes* (right, top and centre). *They are in the spirit of Ernest Montaut (1879–1909) and his school. The spring scene* (bottom, right) *was painted by that other master of motoring art, René Vincent (1879–1936).*

PARIS-VIENNE
1902   GUILLAUME sur DARRACQ

GRAND-PRIX Dieppe   NAZZARO
de l'A·C·F· 1907   sur F·I·A·T·

CE QUE J'AI VU
PAR

than their British and Continental rivals. *Punch* made the point beautifully in a drawing published in 1902. A typical Lanchester is shown meeting a typical De Dion, when the following piece of *Punch* dialogue takes place in the Lanchester's tonneau: *Friend*: 'Going about thirty, are we? But don't you run the risk of being pulled up for exceeding the legal pace?' *Owner*: 'Not in a sober, respectable-looking car like this. Of course, if you go about in a blatant, brass-bound, scarlet-padded, snorting, foreign affair, like *that*, you are bound to be dropped on, no matter how slow you go!'

English drivers preferred to be inconspicuous. The President of the Automobile Club de France, Baron de Zuylen, writing on dress for the Badminton Library in 1900 remarked, no doubt with tongue in cheek, 'Spending part of every year in England I was in a position to know what would and would not be acceptable by British gentlemen. The dress worn by many motorists has been the subject of much irreverent ribaldry. . . .' So instead of shaggy garments, 'Englishmen appear to prefer a coat of Melton cloth lined with fur inside and fitted with a high fur-lined collar.'

In Paris closed cars appeared by the mid 1890s, for while England on the whole was too hilly for the puny engines of the day to cope with closed bodywork, the same was not true of Paris where the steepest hill likely to confront *le tout Paris* was the Avenue des Champs-Elysées. So while the English, despising the decadent fug-loving French, enjoyed motoring as a sport, their neighbours had long since found that the life of a *boulevardier* was immensely simplified if he could drive himself about on his private occasions without coachmen to observe or horses to catch cold. A 'motor brougham' or closed coupé was just the thing for fashionable Paris. When these Proustian vehicles broke down one simply sent for the man. . . . Probably it was only a burner that had blown out, some fluff in the carburetter or a hobnail in one of the tyres.

The roads in the Bois were certainly smooth, but no less certainly the new-fangled pneumatics, having fostered the cycling boom of the 1890s, made things far more comfortable for *tonneau, duc,* and coupé. Road-users everywhere owed a huge debt to the brothers André and Edouard Michelin – and the brothers Michelin owed and still owe an enormous debt to the author of what is perhaps the most famous slogan of all time. *'Le pneu Michelin boit l'obstacle . . . '* ('Michelin

Above: *More Michelin humour, this time by Weiluc, of* Le Rire. *Below: The essence of a 'Roi des Belges' body was the armchair seats, but double-curvature panels were also a feature, whether three-dimensional or, as here, 'tulip'. The car is a 1902–3 four-cylinder Panhard.*

tyres drink up the obstacle') exclaimed some anonymous genius. The coiner of the slogan is unknown but an artist can now receive the credit that is his due for creating the 'Michelin Man' who, at a banquet of nails and broken glass proposes a toast: *'Nunc est bibendum . . .!'* he cries, 'Now let us drink. . . !' And Bibendum he has remained ever since. The artist who dreamed up Bibendum signed his work O'Galop. His real name was Maurice Rossillon. I do not know the date of his birth but he died at Carnac in Brittany on January 2nd 1946, and 'Bibendum' serves as his monument wherever Michelin tyres are sold. The cartoonist Weiluc picked this up in an early drawing in the French humorous paper *Le Rire*. A car has been caught in some floods. 'Never mind', says the passenger, 'Your tyres can drink up the obstacle. . . .'

It was not only pneumatics that made cars more comfortable. Despite the difference in speed early cars had been no better planned and upholstered than harness carriages.

Now one of those not apt to suffer in silence was that king of the Belgians known (unjustly) to Parisians as 'Cléopolde', because of his supposed relationship with Cléo de Mérode. One day this monarch complained that motor car seats were never so comfortable as the chairs in her *salon. 'Eh, bien,'* said she, 'why not have mine copied?' So the King sent for M. Fernand Charles, chief designer of the fashionable Paris coachbuilders, Rheims & Auscher (later known as Rothschild et Cie), measurements were taken and the result was the first *'Roi des Belges'* body in the world, which set the style for touring cars for almost a decade. This four-cylinder Panhard was ready in 1900; each passenger had what amounted to an armchair providing support in all the right places, and the car made a sensation.

The style deserved to catch on. Not only were the individual seats comfortable, but their shape perfectly matched the taste of the period, having the attenuated line and organic curves characteristic of Symbolism and Art Nouveau. The *Zeitgeist* affected engineers and coachbuilders no less than furniture designers; the same inspiration which prompted the first *Roi des Belges* body showed itself also in motoring posters and publicity material. Typical of the period is a wonderfully 'allebolical' painting signed Maurice Ray, entitled *L'hommage allégorique aux automobiles de Dion*, which is described in a later chapter.

Roi des Belges bodies remained popular

The two great allies of early motoring artists were allegory and dust. Both were called in by the Paris goldsmith, Aucoc, author of the Gordon Bennett trophy (left). Jules Forain, poster artist and black-and-white draughtsman, was also a pioneer motorist. Top: *Taking part in the Paris–Berlin race of 1901 (Tourist category) is Forain as seen by his fellow cartoonist, SEM.* Above, *caricatured in* Le Rire, *is the winner, Henry Fournier.*

for ten years, their curves becoming more prominent season by season. The style was a perfect automobile counterpart to that Edwardian ideal the 'fine woman'.

But another international sensation was brewing. Each year since 1895 when Levassor's triumph in the Paris-Bordeaux-Paris race had led to the founding of the Automobile Club de France, this institution had held at least one long-distance event starting from the capital and growing more ambitious each year. The series attained international status with the Paris-Amsterdam race in 1898 and Paris-Ostend in 1899. The big event in 1900 – Paris-Toulouse-Paris – was long but not international, but for 1901 the idea of 'Etoile' races radiating from Paris across Europe was revived, with no less a project than a road race from Paris to Berlin, passing through Sedan and continuing over 687 miles of timed road. The French, always inclined that way, went patriotically car crazy when Achille Fournier's 60 hp Mors proved the winner followed by twelve other French cars before the first German finisher appeared. As Fournier dashed up, checked in and completed a full-speed lap of the trotting track at Potsdam where 20,000 spectators and a reception committee were assembled, a German band played the Marseillaise and Frenchmen everywhere felt that the defeat of 1870 had to some extent been avenged. At least so thought *Le Rire*, which brought out a special number with illustrations by Abel Faivre and M. Radiguet as well as a cartoon of Fournier.

The opening event of Paris-Berlin was

the start of the Tourist class, which attracted forty entrants, ranging from 5 hp voiturette to 35 hp Mercedes. The President of the A.C.F. launched a fashion for touring cars with three rows of seats which became current wear for royalty for a time and were called Baron de Zuylen Phaetons. The Tourists covered the course in eight easy stages, timed to arrive at the same time as the competitors, and were feted everywhere with champagne, mayoral speeches and triumphal arches. Among the drivers was poster artist Jules Forain, one of the *'rois de la caricature'* as well as a motoring enthusiast. This time he was on the receiving end of a cartoonist's pencil: SEM drew him and made the most of it.

Paris-Berlin was undoubtedly the most important fixture of 1901, although other countries including Britain and Italy were becoming interested in the sport. The Giro d'Italia, an ambitious long-distance event, called forth illustrations in the Sunday paper *Domenica del Corriere* by Achille Beltrame, an artist who was to improve and grow livelier over the years. Beltrame could be counted upon to wring the last drop of Boy's Own Paper excitement from his subject. He specialized in disasters involving cars, derailments and sudden deaths. He stayed with the *Corriere* for many years and is remembered for a lively scene in 1913 when a German officer fell out of a staff car on manoeuvres, and for his dramatic drawing of the assassination, in his car, of the Archduke Ferdinand at Sarajevo.

The interest meanwhile was about to shift from the A.C.F.'s own fixtures to a

Top: *Charles Jarrott by 'Spy' (Leslie Ward). When inter-city races became difficult to police, organizers turned to the closed circuit. The first of these events, the Circuit des Ardennes, 1902, was won by the Englishman Charles Jarrott, driving a 40 hp Panhard. His prize was the gold 'medal' shown here.*

new international contest, the Gordon Bennett Trophy. Two editions had passed almost unnoticed in 1900 and 1901, overshadowed by other events; but soon that was all to change when an outsider from Britain captured the Trophy from France. But to return to the beginning: an American enthusiast, James Gordon Bennett whose family owned the *New York Herald* had presented a trophy for international motoring competition, one requirement of which was that every part of the competing cars should be made in the country of origin and that entries should be submitted not by manufacturers but by the Automobile Club of each country concerned.

The prize was to be a challenge trophy, with replica to each winner, and for this stupendous *fin de siècle* creation Mr. James Gordon Bennett went to Aucoc, a Paris goldsmith. 'I want something modern', one can hear him saying, 'but artistic. Something to glorify the automobile and symbolize speed.' And if that is what he asked for, Aucoc certainly did him proud. The period was that of Captain Adrian Jones's *Quadriga*, the chariot of Peace driven four-in-hand by a standing goddess above the arch at Hyde Park Corner in London, and the treatment is rather similar, except that the Gordon-Bennett vehicle is a car of more-than-Symbolist complication. Its passenger is a standing winged goddess, the driver a nude seated on the scuttle-dash, one hand holding aloft the Torch of Progress, the other resting negligently upon the steering wheel of what is probably, beneath the bronze mud, dust and laurels, a Paris-Amsterdam Panhard.

Never was there a finer period piece.

During the first years of the century modern art movements and motoring grew up together. Just as Vlaminck, a musician by training, and André Derain at Chatou discarded all 'save the brass, cymbals and big drum from the orchestra', as Vlaminck put it, and used paint straight from the tube, so car designers piled on the power, becoming mechanical Fauves. The years between 1900 and 1912 have been called the heroic age of motor racing, and there was certainly romance about those desperate inter-city events.

Paris-Berlin having sparked intense commercial and patriotic rivalry, the following year's fixture, Paris-Vienna, put racing on a truly international basis. Although the outright winner was French, Marcel Renault in a 16 hp 'light car' and the next two home were French (Farman, 70 hp Panhard; Edmond, 24 hp Darracq) a splendid showing was made by Count Elliot Zborowski, an amateur driving his own Mercedes. The Count was of Polish origin, with estates in the U.S.A., and this was not all. Concurrently with the first stages of this race was run the 1902 Gordon Bennett Trophy, finishing at Innsbruck. Three cars represented France and there was one British starter, Australian-born S. F. Edge, the Napier concessionaire. To everyone's surprise two of the Frenchmen, Girardot (C. G. V.) and Fournier (Mors) dropped out early and the remaining Frenchman, Chevalier René de Knyff (Panhard) retired with transmission trouble near the end. So the Trophy was awarded, after some argument, to S. F. Edge, whose car had been pushed by spectators and might therefore have been disqualified. Edge was a marvellous publicist and the Napier car became famous; even more important, the French industry, having lost the Gordon Bennett Trophy for the first time, was determined to win it back, especially as another Englishman, Charles Jarrott in a Panhard, won the last event of the season, held for the first time on a closed and guarded course – the Circuit des Ardennes.

Although professing to be bored by the whole business of circuit racing Charles Jarrott does seem to have enjoyed himself, especially after the fourth lap when a bottle of champagne 'handed up at the sharp turn at Bastogne had a very reviving effect'. His account of the race (in *Ten Years of Motors and Motor Racing*, E. Grant Richards, London 1906) is worth quoting: 'At the end of the fifth turn – 60 minutes 32 seconds – I stopped to make sure I had sufficient petrol and water to carry me through, and it was then that I was told Gabriel was sufficiently far ahead to make the race an open one, and I knew that my last fifty-three miles would be a stern chase.

'The dust by this time was fearful, and as we sped on I wondered if I could ever do it. On and on we went, and yet I could see no sign of Gabriel on the Mors. As time went by I became more anxious; and then, reaching a long open stretch of road, we eventually saw, away in the distance, a little speck which I knew must be Gabriel's car. We gradually but steadily gained on him, and then suddenly we shot into another dust zone between a forest of trees. Sitting in the dust, unable to see a thing, and yet pushing the car at top speed, it seemed incredible that we should come through without accident. There was no question now of slowing at corners or taking things steadily; it was only a question of who was to finish first. Then Gabriel's car loomed up in the dust before us and suddenly slowed down, and I narrowly escaped dashing into it from behind. Gabriel had stopped with a broken chain and we were alone, only seven kilometers from the finish, and we thundered down into Bastogne amid great excitement . . .'

The prize awarded by the Belgian Automobile Club for the winner of the event was, in Jarrott's words, 'a beautifully designed little gold medal, which I treasure amongst my most valued possessions at the present day.' Now, a quarter of a century after Charles Jarrott's death, the little medal has returned to Belgium as part of the de Beauffort Collection, a fine example of goldsmith's work which makes a change from the usual chalice or sculpture.

The 1903 Season opened with the most ambitious of all the *courses à l'étoile*, Paris-Madrid, which became notorious as the first big fixture in which drivers and spectators were killed.

The first stage, from Paris to Bordeaux ran over the fastest and straightest road in Europe and the day was hot. Dust from the untarred surface made overtaking hazardous and sometimes rose so high that drivers were steering by the tops of the trees, as Jarrott had done in the Ardennes. Pre-race publicity had been good, and the public turned out to watch. Policing and marshalling were bad. Several drivers crashed fatally, including Marcel Renault, and instead of continuing to Irun, Vittoria and Madrid, the race was halted at Bordeaux. Some newspapers called it the Race of Death; others foretold the death of

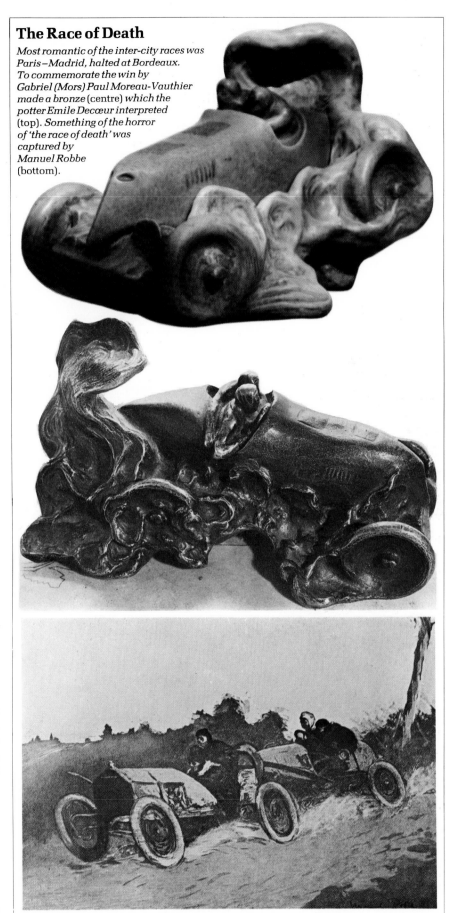

The Race of Death

Most romantic of the inter-city races was Paris–Madrid, halted at Bordeaux. To commemorate the win by Gabriel (Mors) Paul Moreau-Vauthier made a bronze (centre) which the potter Emile Decœur interpreted (top). Something of the horror of 'the race of death' was captured by Manuel Robbe (bottom).

The Chasseloup-Laubat trophy, a bronze plaque by André Falize, went to Léon Théry, winner of the French 'Elimination Races' of 1904 and 1905. It was afterwards presented by the car manufacturer, Brasier, to the Automobile Club de France.

Very keen and successful in early races was the Belgian, Baron Pierre de Caters, here represented in a tiny (3-inch) bronze Mercedes with a special radiator cowl, signed Löder. The crouching attitude is due not to artistic exaggeration but to the need to breathe and to reduce wind-resistance. Below it is a beautifully detailed bronze model (length 6 inches), cast by the lost-wax process and representing a de Dietrich with duc body (Amédée Bollée licence).

racing. As usual Authority panicked. competitors, engines quenched, were towed to the railway by horses. As usual the scaremongers were wrong. Within a month the next important race was being held, the second Circuit des Ardennes. What is more, two weeks after the Belgian race everyone in motoring converged on the Curragh outside Dublin for the Gordon Bennett, which the Royal Automobile Club had staged on this nominally British soil because road-racing in England was not allowed. Edge was defending; France and Germany were both determined to win this time.

The race's international flavour was greater than ever, for it was Jenatzy, a Belgian in a German Mercedes, who won back the French-made American trophy from its British holder. Panhards were second and third, a Mors fourth and a Mercedes fifth. Germany therefore had the privilege of staging the next year's Gordon Bennett and the French, thoroughly stung, vowed to win it back.

All this activity excited artists both amateur and professional, and set them to ponder the problems of speed and movement. Aesthetically humble though these explorations of spatial and dimensional relationships may have been compared with the theorizing and experiment of schools like the Vorticists

and Futurists (whose turn would soon come) they make an interesting study in themselves.

There was an artist named Manuel Robbe born in 1872 who seems to have taken an interest in the subject from very early days. James Barron in his exhibition at the Bethnal Green Museum in London in 1974 showed a dappled Impressionist aquatint by him of a forecar in a riverside lane, in which an impression of movement is conveyed by the glint of light on wheels and brasswork. Five or six years after this work was produced Robbe turns up as one of those moved by the tragedies of Paris-Madrid. His is a dark satanic painting of cars overtaking at close quarters, now in the Musée de la Voiture at Compiègne. The scene is set on a downhill slope and the spectator sees a Mercedes almost in profile, and an overtaking car which is hard to identify as its bonnet is already hidden by its opponent's back wheels. The road is an appropriate sand colour and little spurts of dust come from the wheels. Robbe uses sombre colours, silhouetting the first car against a dark green background and the overtaker mainly against the sky; drivers hunch forward and mechanics perch precariously on the floorboards 'en lapin' as the saying was. But the drama comes from an unusual perspective: for although the cars must be

similar in size the leader is small, the overtaker large, so that the latter appears to be swallowing up his adversary. The treatment is broad and although painted in oils the scene might almost be a lino-cut.

This painting has another peculiarity and one wonders how many viewers observed it at the time. The wheels and the cars themselves lean forward, a deliberate distortion much used by later portrayers of speed. When Manuel Robbe employed it in 1903 he was deliberately adopting a photographic technique. Racing cars even at Paris-Madrid speeds (and Gabriel the winner *averaged* 65 mph to Bordeaux, so he must have been doing over eighty most of the time) move too fast for the eye to observe much detail, but not too fast for the camera. By 'panning' – swinging to keep the object in the centre of the viewfinder – photographers can 'stop' the car with a relatively long exposure at the expense of a blurred background and spokes, both of which enhance the impression of speed. But press cameras of the period used large plates (about 12×15 cm) and a focal-plane shutter consisting of a roller-blind with a slit which travelled vertically across the plate. Thus, in the small fraction of time during which the slit moved over the plate the car itself had moved, so that in the finished print the car appears to lean forward and the wheels are oval. The effect was rather dramatic, and as even racegoers based their impressions on photographs in the newspapers, and photographs looked like this, it was thought that this must be how racing cars looked.

There must be many other souvenirs of Paris-Madrid, if only because the shape of Gabriel's *Dauphin* Mors was so modernistic in its day and its performance so utterly remarkable; it was the sort of model that Goss china might well have continued making into the 1920s. Be that as it may, it inspired the *fin de siècle* sculptor Paul Moreau-Vauthier to make it into a bronze, a Rodinesque piece in which the dust in its wake looks unfortunately like washing. This bronze appeared also in polychrome stoneware by the well-known French ceramist Emile Decoeur (1876–1953), when it was more successful as a box for trinkets or cigarettes. It was used by the Bethnal Green Museum in London on the cover of their catalogue for the James O. Barron exhibition. Paul Moreau-Vauthier was responsible also for an allegorical work to commemorate Blériot's first cross-Channel aeroplane flight in 1909. Maître Hervé Poulain states that Vauthier was a specialist in funerary

sculpture and may therefore have had an interest in vehicles driving *à tombeau ouvert*, or as we might say 'Hell bent'. Another famous French ceramist of this period also modelled cars: Adrien-Pierre Dalpayrat (1844–1910). He was famous for a uniquely coloured glaze, known as *rouge* Dalpayrat; his great days were in Art Deco.

Following Edge's win in the Gordon Bennett of 1902, the privilege of holding the race went to the Royal Automobile Club, which, as we have seen, was forced to hold it in Ireland since road racing in England was illegal. The effort was patriotically vain: the race was won by Jenatzy, the Belgian 'Red Devil' with a forked rufous beard, driving a German car. The Mercedes victory therefore took the next year's event to the Fatherland, where the Kaiser and his enthusiast brother Prince Henry, pulled out all the picturesque stops. A hilly demanding circuit was chosen in the Taunus mountains, near the fashionable resort of Homburg, a favourite spot with the international set which gave its name to the hat otherwise known as a trilby.

A Roman fort stood near the start and finish line, and so His Imperial and Royal Highness Wilhelm II, Emperor of Germany, had the grandstands built in the classical manner. He was also to be there in person, to witness a German victory.

But France, too, was very much in the hunt. The problem there was not finding cars, but rather deciding which make or makes should represent the French industry. When no fewer than ten firms requested to enter, the A.C.F. held an Eliminating Trial, taking the form of a race over a circuit in the Massif Central near Clermont Ferrand, headquarters of the Michelin Tyre Company. Every component, under the regulations, had to be made in the country of origin.

The trials were won by Léon Théry in a Richard-Brasier, and it was he too who disappointed the Kaiser by winning the big event for France, in spite of the Roman fort and Imperial trappings. The 1905 event was therefore to be held on French soil, and if a surfeit of competitors entered, *Eliminatoires* would be held as before.

During 1905 the French, dissatisfied with the Gordon Bennett as it did not allow them full play, announced that win or lose they would not enter in 1906. Instead the smart and powerful Automobile Club de France from its frontage on the Place de la Concorde published regulations for a race of its own, to be known as the Grand Prix of the A.C.F., and this became the premier

Pierre Dalpayrat (1844–1910) was alone in obtaining a particular coloured glaze, the 'rouge Dalpayrat', *seen in these two ceramic pieces.*

race of the season except during the slump years of 1909, 1910 and 1911.

The Gordon Bennett series provided work for large numbers of artists, who had taken to the race gradually. In the days before Edge's luck in 1902 and the ensuing Gallic frenzy, no motoring paper had had money to spend on artistic coverage. All they could run to was a reporter, some photographs, and sometimes local men lurking with sketch-pads.

In Italy an early example of one of these lurkers was Achille Beltrame, and there is in the A.F.C. a wash drawing by Arnold Moreaux of Achille Fournier on the line at Champigny, being flagged away at the start of Paris-Berlin. The starter's flag is raised, a dog is barking at the front near-side wheel (reminding us that cycle-shops did a brisk trade in breech-loading 'Vélo-dog' pistols), and the atmosphere is static, as though the wind had dropped. One has the impression that this is 'motion recollected in tranquillity', in other words based on a photograph. Manuel Robbe's painting of the Paris-Madrid must have been actually sketched by the road-side, however much it may owe to the focal-plane shutter.

At this time of aspidistras and overloaded mantelpieces there was quite a vogue for bronze racing-cars, most of them unsigned and usually French. Bronzes of the Belle Epoque could be very beautiful; they could also look something life toffee, and this we feel applies to the Chasseloup-Laubat Plate, a plaque modelled by André Falize (b. 1872) which was won by Théry's Brasier in the French Eliminating Trials

1904–1905 and is now in the A.C.F. in Paris. The twisty road and mountains are reasonable Art Nouveau landscape, but the car itself might be a pastry-cook's model.

Editors trained during the heroic age of racing had a slang word for slapdash brushwork, especially when this was used for dust or draperies shrouding mechanical details which an artist preferred not to draw. They called it, for some forgotten reason, 'pork'.

A commercial artist rather prone to 'pork' in his lithographs of racing cars was Harry Eliott, no doubt because he understood their mechanism less well than he understood hunting or night-clubs, two of his other specialities. When motoring became popular during mid-Edwardian times a number of sporting artists were put on to cars with greater or less success, like the *Punch* man Lance Thackeray, and, perhaps before 1900 another specialist in fox-hunting, Stuart Travis.

The French Gordon Bennett races in 1905 were to be a high time for the artist who happened to be keen on cars. Eliminating Trials and the race itself were held on the same course as before, in the Auvergne near the Puy de Dôme, and sufficiently remote and rural to make spectating a delight.

Some pages from a sketchbook of a young local artist, Gaston Maurié (1873–1912) now in the Poulain Collection set the scene wonderfully well: the loose dusty roads, the flags, the *services d'ordre* in white-trousered Sunday best, the informal atmosphere. This was casual even by French provincial motor sporting

André Névil's rather stilted oil painting of the 1905 Gordon Bennett races in the Auvergne contrasts with Gaston Maurié's Impressionist treatment of the Eliminating Races shown opposite.

standards, as it turned out, although intentions had been good. Communications were to have been maintained by telephone, but peasants stole the wire to bind up their hay. Then the organizers, very progressively, tried the new-fangled wireless telegraphy, but this could not be made to work. Perhaps the mountains did not encourage reception.

The Maurié paintings are full of life and sparkle. Painted in gouache mainly in the pale blues and mauves loved by Marie Laurencin, they are built Impressionistically of light. Evidently painted at the Eliminating Trials, they tell us that car No. 7, a 17-litre 130 hp De Dietrich (190×150 mm bore and stroke) entrusted to Fernand Gabriel, hero of Paris-Madrid, was painted white with red running gear and that Achille Fournier's 18.8-litre 130 hp Hotchkiss (185×175 mm bore and stroke) was light blue with a brass radiator. Fournier wore white overalls, Gabriel's were brown. Maurié's treatment is gay, airy and Impressionist, the compositions are clever and the human figures well drawn; but he did not rely on high-speed glimpses; he had obviously been round the Paddock, for every bracket and spring-hanger is in its right place.

Once again Léon Théry won, so it was he who led the French team in the Gordon Bennett itself. At least two oil paintings of the big race survive in modern collections. On the great day André Névil must have been on hand to see Théry's fourth consecutive win, for he signs and dates his work

'5 juill. '05'. Was the artist with the party in the large red touring car which occupies the left of the canvas? Opposite, little knots of spectators are grouped on the rocky hillside, while on the verge of the road itself stand – casual as ever – a motorcyclist and a soldier leaning upon his rifle. And as Théry's blue Brasier speeds past raising the dust a small dog dashes into the road. A true incident, maybe, perhaps one invented to give drama and scale.

Each of the four laps measured some 80 miles and passed through some of the hilliest, twistiest roads in the Massif Cèntral.

Henri-Charles Willems, painter of a large oil now in the Musée des Arts et Métiers, Paris, did well to choose an uphill hairpin as his viewpoint, evidently raised slightly above the road. The moment shown must have come early in the race before Vincenzo Lancia's Fiat lost its water, and while it was pressing Théry really hard. The Fiat is right on his tail, and the Frenchman is at full stretch, on full left lock with his hands crossed, outside wheel sliding and nearside well off the road, while the mechanic

her *en automobiliste*. In this group stands the solidly bourgeois figure of Monsieur Brasier, of Automobiles Richard-Brasier, builders of Théry's car.

Following Théry's 1904 success Brasier and his advertising manager must have cast around for a suitable poster artist. They chose Belléry Desfontaines who not only did them proud but produced what is really an anthology of Art Nouveau, even to the lettering and the tenuously curving foliage below linking the two four-leafed clovers which formed the trademark. But the centrepiece is Léon Théry's racer. The car rushes across the poster, its rear half

leans out, placing his weight where it is needed most. Dust shows that the Brasier is sliding, and also helps to silhouette the Fiat against a light background. As a painter Willems was old-fashioned, but this big canvas, 48×80 inches, is a valuable motoring document and one which would have appealed to racing people.

This 1905 event was the last Gordon Bennett motor race, the end of an epoch. The whole of motoring Europe had converged upon Clermont Ferrand, and with them, naturally, MICH of *La Vie Parisienne*. We know some of the notabilities in the Paddock that morning thanks to a cartoon of his, an amusing gallery of characters including the spade-bearded De Knyff and the hour-glass Madame du Gast, who had driven so well and so fast in the early long-distance races, and who would have finished well up in Paris-Madrid had she not stopped to help one of the injured. Perhaps somewhere there is a portrait of enveloped in dust and its front wheels almost dusted into the ground. Théry hunches urgently over the wheel while from the front of the car emerges ectoplasmically a prone Goddess of Speed, her hair *en nouille* forming the 'speed lines' which were one of the early discoveries of the motoring artist.

Was it this poster, one wonders, that inspired Polak, the sculptor who dreamed up the Coppa della Velocità? The race for this trophy formed the climax to a Motor Week at Brescia, and proved the fastest event of its age. The animator of this meeting was Cavaliere Vincenzo Florio, the wealthy Sicilian enthusiast whose name was to become so well known in motor racing. The 1905 race, over a 104-mile circuit from Brescia to Cremona and Mantua and back to Brescia, proved the fastest of its period, 312 miles at 65 mph, 'and the Coppa della Velocità itself' (*coppa* meaning not cup but trophy) is motoring Art Nouveau at its most lyrical and most naïve. On a long silver plinth stands a racing car with stationary wheels, crewed by a pair of winged *putti*, crouched to their work and engaged in driving their steed as fast as possible up the skirts of the *grande horizontale* who forms a forward extension of the car and whose trailing gown eddies upwards behind the car like a breaking wave. It is a charming piece, examples of which still survive.

All the same when, the following year, Florio instituted his famous Targa Florio series of races in the Madonian Mountains of Sicily, whose roads excelled even those of the Auvergne in tortuosity, the Cavaliere went to probably the best man in Paris, René Lalique (1860–1945). Not yet specialized in glass, Lalique was already famous for his Symbolist *bijouterie*, semi-precious adornments of gold, silver, bronze, mother of pearl and enamel that Alphonse Mucha might well have designed for Sarah Bernhardt or for one of those mythical ladies in an early automobile poster. For Signor Florio, Lalique created a trophy which anyone would have been proud to win, a rectangular *targa* (which means plaque or plate and is still the word for number-plates on cars) in bronze, carrying a bas-relief of a racing car against a Sicilian background, the sky suggested in blue enamel. For the following year Lalique made a similar plaque but added a symbolic flight of blue swallows, anticipating Maeterlinck's *Blue Bird* by a couple of years, and also some clumps of flowers in polychrome enamel. How long Lalique continued his series of Florio plaques is not clear, but it may be mentioned for the record that by the 1920s, when Lalique was specializing in glass, Florio chose the artist Henry Dropsy, Lalique's junior by twenty-five years.

A triumph of Art Nouveau, the *Coppa della Velocità* (otherwise *Coppa Florio*) went as a challenge trophy to the winner of the race which formed the climax of the annual Motor Week at Brescia. It was commissioned by Vincenzo Florio and bears the signature 'Polak'. The outstretched arms originally held a laurel wreath.

A Varied and Belle Epoque

Ernest Montaut and his school; early poster artists and painters

FROM THE AIRY GRACE of a swallow to the reality of an Edwardian racing car is a far cry; consider the vital statistics of Léon Théry's Brasier. Carrying no bodywork except a pair of bucket seats with a petrol tank behind, it was practically all bonnet; and under this bonnet was nothing but engine, a vast four-cylinder side-valve with 160 mm bore and 140 mm stroke, giving a capacity of 11½ litres, roughly ten times the size of a small family car's engine today. Yet the Brasier was not big by Gordon Bennett standards: De Dietrich engines were 190 by 150 mm, giving 17 litres – more than twice the capacity of a Rolls-Royce Corniche. These cars ran on tyres more than a yard in diameter and the driver's eyes were on the level with those of a man walking. Chain drive was used and to save weight only a three-speed gearbox, for this entire monster was limited by the regulations to a maximum of 1007 kilogrammes, the same as, for example, an Austin Maxi. These cars would be doing about 100 mph downhill, and the metal-to-metal brakes would be unlikely to last the course. Roads were dusty and loose and heavily cambered, so that cars would be sliding most of the time. Heroic racing indeed, requiring heroic treatment.

This treatment was provided by a young artist named Ernest Montaut (1879–1909). In fact one could almost say – if the litres

were not there to disprove it – that the Heroic Age was Montaut's own creation. The moment was right for popular motorcar art. Car business was booming. Factories were selling more cars than they could make, and showrooms were being built on every hand. Some had been there for some time, like the palatial London premises of C. S. Rolls & Company in Conduit Street where the Hon. Charles had been selling Panhards for some time before his meeting with F. H. Royce. The Rolls-Royce show rooms are still there, but, alas, the two-foot squares of black and white marble with which C.S.R. covered the floor have recently been carpeted over. Perhaps it does not matter now, but they were most useful once: the Hon. Charles, it is said, used often to win bets that he could guess the wheelbase of any car that happened to be in the showroom, and these slabs may have helped.

It is doubtful whether a Montaut print ever graced the walls of that Conduit Street car shop, but Montaut's spirited designs must have decorated more showroom walls, private garages and enthusiasts' studies than any other productions of his time. Wall space was plentiful and these big coloured lithographs were decorative, dramatic and very much in the spirit of the age. The Belle Epoque was a time of heroes and hero worship, and invention. People took pride in, identified with and took

Facing page: *In* Un Match Moderne, *a race between a Renault G.P. car and pusher biplane, two of Ernest Montaut's specialities are on display: drama and atmosphere. His techniques for representing speed have influenced artists ever since. Above is a window based on the same Montaut lithograph by the Californian stained-glass artist, Paul Marioni (born 1941).*

credit for new inventions like telephones, phonographs, airships, aeroplanes and motor cars.

Technical subjects require technical knowledge, and Montaut certainly understood cars, what is more he invented or popularized nearly all the tricks for rendering speed except that of blurring the spokes to show that a wheel is going round. The first to do that was Velasquez, not for 'wheelspin' as we know it, but in painting a spinning-wheel.

Montaut's tricks could form the subject of a minor thesis. His cars are always identifiable, and the impression of speed may come from any part of the picture. Smoke and dust were his allies, but these never degenerated into 'pork' to hide the bits that mattered; Montaut makes it clear whether a car has shaft drive like a Renault or chain drive like most of the others. His characters act out the speed. Drivers peer intently down the road as men do when driving fast; or they glance hurriedly at their instruments. They hold the wheel at 'twenty-to-four' with their palms upwards and elbows down as was necessary with the big cars and high-ratio steering of those days. Riding-mechanics look round for pursuers, tap their driver on the shoulder to draw his attention, pump-up pressure in the fuel tank or simply hang grimly on. Most effective of all they glance back at the artist as they pass. Montaut is sparing of 'speed lines', probably considering them too easy, but he allows the road to tell its own story and sometimes dramatizes the trees, which sway as though they too were

travelling fast, and scudding clouds occasionally add to the effect. A device he found useful, and which many later artists copied, was to light the car from behind so that it cast a shadow in front, leading it towards the viewer and sometimes right out of the picture. Many Montaut drawings are semi-vignetted in this way, most of the composition being contained within ruled margins but certain elements being allowed to escape.

Spectators sometimes contribute to the scene although less often with Montaut than in the work of some of his followers. Occasionally he permits himself a speed symbol in the corner of the mount. His 1908 Grand Prix Renault has such a symbol, a swallow. In *Moscow-St. Petersbourg, 1907*, a head-on view of a De Dietrich hurtling across the Steppes with a sunset sky behind and dramatic hard shadow in front, the symbol is an affrighted Cossack. Dramatically this is one of the best of Montaut's racing prints, an excellent likeness of a De Dietrich, from the characteristic radiator to the pile of spare tyres behind, the whole thing rushing straight out of the frame. 'Yes, very disquieting,' remarked a Vintage enthusiast when shown it for the first time. 'The car has no track-rod. In fact no steering-connexions of any kind. I'm going to get out of the way!' Both he and the artist were right. The car is indeed without steering, but its attitude shows where it is going, and too much detail, as in a portrait or cartoon, would spoil the effect.

Montaut, like Robbe in the Paris-Madrid

Ernest Montaut invented many tricks in the cause of speed. Perhaps his bending of the car to suggest cornering was not his best brainwave, but the Fauve colour is dramatic, and the 'speed lines', not yet a cliché, anticipated Futurism.

Ernest Montaut's lithographs, like that shown (above right) of François Szisz in the 1906 Grand Prix, were widely sold in France, Britain and the United States. His original drawings and watercolours however are published here for the first time, through the kindness of Maître Hervé Poulain. The drawing (above left) is the sketch for one of the best-known lithographs, Arthur Duray (De Dietrich) winning Moscow–St. Petersburg, 1907. Note the vignette of a frightened cossack, inserted for dramatic effect. With this delicate drawing the bold gouache (top right) entitled Le Feu de la Course *forms a stunning contrast.*

painting already discussed, sometimes drew on camera techniques. He knew that the human eye could not 'stop' a car in full flight, that only a lens could do that, and that we tend to intellectualize our impressions, basing what we take to be memories on photographs in the press. Montaut sometimes distorted the wheels as though by a focal-plane shutter, sometimes he 'panned' so that the background was not sharp, often the foreground is sketchily blurred or vignetted – in photographic terms out of focus. Another camera trick Montaut had picked up was the effect of the wide-angle lens. He often based his foreshortening on this, showing the front wheels much larger than the back. Other tricks of distortion which he explored, such as bending the car downwards as it breasted a hill or bending it banana-wise to exaggerate a corner may be written off as unsuccessful experiments. Be that as it may, no collection of motoring art would be complete without its Montaut. Original

prints are not hard to find, and not very expensive. Also modern reproductions are being made, an indication that he is now considered an artist of some importance.

Of E. Montaut himself almost nothing has been published until now. Even his first name is sometimes erroneously quoted as Edouard, and he has been dismissed as a *petit maître*. Recently however Mᵉ. Hervé Poulain has made contact with the artist's family and it is possible to re-assess his achievement in the light of sketches published here for the first time. Ernest Montaut was born in 1879 and fell ill and died in his thirty-first year, leaving a wife and one-year-old child. Before him there had been virtually no artists of motor racing; he had to invent all the techniques, and it is clear that he was receptive to all the movements under discussion at the time. His lighting can be Impressionist, his trees, swaying to the passage of a car, take on Symbolist curves. He is not afraid to colour like a Fauve. Ernest Montaut was as ready to distort in the cause of duty as the Post-Impressionists, and like the Futurist style

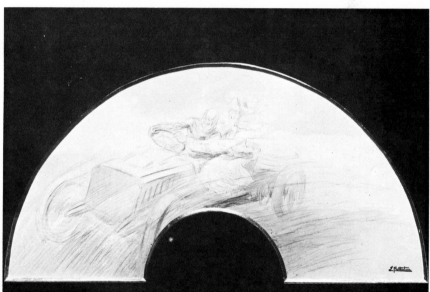

Left: *An example of Montaut's borrowing of photographic techniques, in this case that of the short-focus lens, this lithograph shows a Renault Grand Prix car of 1908. The swallow is a form of 'sympathetic magic', heightening the impression of speed.* Bottom left: *Squared up for enlargement, this dramatic painting was a sketch for a poster advertising Clement military vehicles and aero-engines.* Below: *This charming little gouache sketch for a fan must have appealed to Montaut's wife, Marguerite. It was called* Ivresse de la Vitesse.

still incubating at the time of his early death on August 9th 1909 he knew how to combine the present tense with the future and the future perfect showing what is, what will be and what will have been. Montaut seems also to have worked in a bewildering variety of styles, from boldest woodcut to most delicate watercolour, some of the latter, in which airships pass over a sunny landscape with cars, being almost ethereal.

The artist's original line drawings were reproduced lithographically in two sizes, the larger ones 18 inches by 36, the smaller about 9 inches by 12. The majority of subjects were in the long low 'marine' format, a few – like *Un Match Moderne*, an aeroplane racing a car through a mountain pass – vertical. The large prints were sold loose or framed in a dark-oak ogee moulding; the smaller ones could be bought separately or in an attractive album, pierced and tied with green cord, called *10 Ans de Courses 1897–1907*, which appeared in 1908. By that time Montaut was allied with the lithographic publishers M. Mabileau and a firm called Montaut-Mabileau (*Estampes, affiches, publicité par l'image*) existed with premises at 84 rue d'Amsterdam in Paris and London representation by Leo. Ripault & Co., 64a Poland Street, W.1. Their trademark was an attractive Art Nouveau nude with a Gibson Girl hairstyle inspecting the print of a Grand Prix Renault, the whole contained in an oblong

Bottom: *Montaut made several versions of this dramatic moment for Gabriel during the 1904 Vanderbilt Cup race on Long Island, altering details of the locomotive, and the title. One version is captioned 'Gabriel and his Lorraine-Dietrich narrowly avoid a distressing encounter at a level crossing.' Made by Tiffany & Co., the New York jewellers, the bronze medal, measuring 1⅜ inches by 1¼, was awarded to the winner; a similar medal formed part of the big Challenge Cup itself. The inscription reads: 'Challenge Cup presented by W. K. Vanderbilt, Jr., to the American Automobile Association under deed of gift to be raced for yearly by cars under 1000 miles. Second race in America October 14th 1905 won by France, Darracq car 80 hp, driven by Victor Hemery, time 9 hours 36 minutes 8 seconds. Distance 283 miles.'*

black border. Probably the album was originally to have been called *10 Ans 1898–1908*, because the first in the series is Charron's 1898 Pari-Amsterdam Panhard, but Montaut added a hasty sketch of Levassor's 1895 triumph in his summary late manner, and numbered it 0 in the stone. The number of plates in an album seems to have varied from twenty-five to more than thirty.

Unlike Edwardian cameramen, Montaut lived in a world of colour – vivid cars in a vivid landscape, sometimes fanciful, sometimes naturalistic. For a long while these Montaut prints were assumed to be colour lithographs, but on looking closely one finds that only the lines are lithographic. It has also been suggested that the colours were applied by 'the *pochoir* process'; but this simply means stencilling, and the lack of hard edges, the use of washes, the intricacy of the colouring and the fact that the tints are always in register rather preclude this. Close inspection suggests they were hand coloured by professional colourists working freehand; the paint is watercolour, heightened here and there with white or pale blue body-colour, e.g., on wheel spokes and dust clouds. The colourists seem to have pleased themselves as to which colours to use; at least three completely different versions of the Moscow-St. Petersburg are known: an all-beige De Dietrich, a yellow car with red radiator, and a pinkish car with scarlet radiator and crimson under the wings. The sky and landscape are handled completely differently in each case although the outlines are identical.

It seems likely that second editions were sometimes drawn, and that Montaut was

published also in America. A very dramatic Montaut of Fernand Gabriel in the 1904 Vanderbilt Cup race on Long Island is evidence of this:

'When Mr. James Gordon Bennett instituted the trophy which bears his name,' wrote the late Gerald Rose in 1908 'he gave an impetus to the industry which was of incalculable value. In the same way another American, Mr. W. K. Vanderbilt, jun. himself a racing driver of the highest ability, presented a trophy to the American Automobile Association in January 1904.' The first two races for the trophy were to be held on American soil, and the first of these attracted a very good European as well as an American entry, including a Clement Bayard car driven by Albert Clement which, except for the 'hairy caterpillar' gilled-tube radiator was so modern in its lines that it would not have looked out of place in 1914. The Vanderbilt Cup itself, though large and handsome, was disappointing compared with the baroque splendours of the Gordon Bennett Trophy and the overwhelmingly *modern style* beguilements of the Coppa Florio. It was a large chalice, richly rimmed with laurel and bearing a well-executed, rather photographic bas-relief of a racing car at speed.

In the 1904 Vanderbilt Cup race on Long Island, level-crossings gave trouble; some cars broke springs and Fernand Gabriel in the 60 hp De Dietrich just managed not to dead-heat with a train. The caption to the Montaut print reads: 'Gabriel et sa Lorraine-Dietrich risquent de peu la fâcheuse rencontre à un passage à niveau'. Different prints show two versions of the Long Island Railroad locomotive which Gabriel narrowly missed, one evidently correcting the original version.

By 1914 Montaut had set up his own

firm, listed as Montaut et Cie, *Estampes sportives*, 7 avenue des Monts-Clairs, Colombes (Les Vallées), Seine. His work was evidently high regarded, for the Paris magazine *Les Hommes du Jour* devoted a special number to him in a series which included such poster artists as Steinlen, Léandre, Willette, Guillaume and Chéret.

Montaut's wife Marguerite was also an artist and a very adequate draughtsman of cars, indeed there are Montaut drawings dated 1914 which have been taken for Ernest's own work, although on close reading the signature is found to be 'M. Montaut'. Following Ernest's death the business was carried on by Mabileau et Cie, and a number of additional artists taken on as the business expanded into aeronautics, motor cycling, increased car publicity and speed boats. These workers included André Nevil, whose signature is sometimes read 'A. W. Nevil' and who has been noted in connexion with the Gordon-Bennet races; M. Campion, Geo. Bric, Léon Dufort and Roowy, whose colourful poster of a comic astronomer mistaking a Diatto car for a thunderbolt is worth a place in any poster collection. None of these artists seem to figure in the biographical lists, and neither does a mysterious figure named Gamy, who seems to have joined the firm in 1909. Like Montaut, Gamy painted in a number of styles. Some of the work, especially the aeroplanes, which remain convincingly aloft, and the people who are both well dressed and well observed, is rather more than good illustration, although some of the cars remain disarmingly crude. Nothing is on record about Gamy, but a suspicion begins to form that Gamy may possibly be an anagram of Magy, for Marguerite Montaut.

During the Montaut years, another French automobile specialist, René Vincent, was at work making humorous drawings, illustrations, catalogues and posters. However, as his output extended from the early days until the 1930s, his work will be discussed in a later chapter.

Motorcars during the *Belle Epoque* were not all racing monsters à la Montaut, but varied all the way from the economical 'one-lung' 6 hp De Dion to majestic limousines of 40, 50 and even 60 horsepower, and electric broughams which under the patronage of King Edward VII rapidly became the thing in London, as in Paris. Hyde Park, like the Bois, was a place for smart cars; cars driven by chauffeurs earning perhaps as much as two pounds a week but costing their owners up to a thousand pounds a year in tyres.

One of the earliest posters advertising a motor race, this one is by Georges Gaudy who, like the race in question, was Belgian. The use of speed lines at this date is interesting. Below: Pair of panels by a French primitive painter, c. 1900

Motoring art at this time was as varied as the cars themselves. One of the great disappointments is that the Douanier Rousseau does not seem to have put cars into his paintings: boats, aeroplanes and charming little dirigible airships decorate his pictures but so far as I know not a single car. Other primitives however were busy, like the Sunday painter responsible for the pair of panels shown on this page. This man evidently knew his motorcars and the fact that he chose steel panels – perhaps enamel advertising signs – instead of canvas or board suggests that he was perhaps in the motor or coach-building trades.

By contrast the establishment at first went in for that pretty mixture of allegory and monumentality which, half a century before, had led the Prince Consort to refuse to allow a statue of himself at the 1851 Exhibition, remarking that there were enough bad monuments already and he saw no reason to be laughed at unduly. Allegory, though, was not a laughing matter when De Dion Boutons were young, but an excuse to draw half-draped models disguised as the Goddess of Speed. An early poster by one Maurice Ray (probably a pseudonym) is called *Hommage allégorique aux automobiles de Dion* and pulls out all the stops: a winged goddess in a Roman chariot holds aloft a 6 hp engine, flanked by two allegorical personages while below, deliciously drawn like a jewel by Sarah Bernhardt's favourite artist Mucha, lies another goddess with peacock wings.

The foliage flanking the design is purest Art Nouveau, the fern-like curves of which had probably as much influence on early car body design as King Leopold's Louis XVI armchair. The Automobile Club de France, fashionably sited amongst the monuments of the Place de la Concorde, showed preference for allegory in its posters for the Salon, when with the example of Lautrec and the Nabis before them they might have been expected to be bold.

Paris had long been the home of the poster. When the old buildings and narrow streets of mediaeval Paris had been swept away by Napoleon III's new broom, many people found Baron Haussmann's new Paris a pretty drab place, with its wide impersonal boulevards as yet unshaded by trees, and its chilly neo-Mansard façades, apparently bought by the mile. But there was one saving grace, the art of Jules Chéret, and the little round kiosks called *colonnes d'affiches* put up to receive them. Born in 1838, a Parisian of Parisians, Jules Chéret was drawing letters for a lithographer by the time he was thirteen. In 1866, with backing from Rimmel, the perfumier, he set up in Paris after ten years spent in London studying the new techniques of colour lithography. His posters covered the drab new town with coruscating pretty girls, a whirl of gaiety advertising everything under the sun. Crying *'Toujours les femmes et les rires!'*, he was incessantly inventing new toilettes for his blonde models, his Chérettes as Paris called them.

Chéret de-prettified Watteau and brought him up to date; he flung paint around with more-than-Impressionist abandon, and he strongly influenced Lautrec. A Belgian critic was close to the mark when he called Chéret *'Ce Tiepolo des rues'.* He certainly made one motoring poster – a Chérette in delicious apricot motoring coat overtaking another, more sombre chauffeuse thanks, no doubt, to the *'Benzo-Moteur, essence spéciale pour automobiles'* on which her car is running. This work must date from the late 1890s, for in 1900 Chéret forsook posters for easel painting. In 1893 the ancestor to the Paris Salon, then called simply the Salon du Cycle, had not been exactly inspired in its advertising, although no doubt patriotism was a selling point at the time. Drawn by E. Clouet, the poster simply showed *poilus* from the cycle corps pedalling away from their bivouac towards *la gloire* – the contemporary equivalent of silently descending paratroops done in the style of the illustrated papers. J.-L. Forain made an elegant drawing for the following year's salon that was a great improvement, and as the century turned and horses deserted the fashionable carriage, manufacturers such as De Dion Bouton commissioned Symbolist publicity like the Maurice Ray already discussed. Jules Chéret meanwhile had been rewarded with the Légion d'Honneur 'for creating a new branch of art, by applying art to commercial and industrial printing'. The A.C.F. were saving Georges Rochegrosse (1859–1938), master of Roman orgies, the Parisian Alma Tadema or Fortunino Matania of his day, to paint a poster for their Ballet Automobile des Nations at the Opéra in 1903. So, exploring every boulevard and leaving no lithographic stone unturned, they set about finding a substitute.

In view of the Automobile Club's interest in racing it would have been at least historically appropriate if they had chosen for their Salon posters the artist who probably drew the first motor racing poster of all. This was a Belgian racing cyclist named Georges Gaudy, born at Saint-Josse-Ten-Noode in 1872, who made a poster for the A.C. de Belgique's Brussels–Spa race in the summer of 1898, and one cannot get much earlier than that. His bold lithographic design, in beige, bright blue, dark blue and green is purest Art Nouveau down to the lettering, landscape background and mosaics. It shows what might well be a Benz victoria crewed and psychically controlled by Chronos, or Old Father Time, scythe in one hand, hour-glass in the other, crouching forward, his hair and robes blowing in the wind: a splendid im-

Facing page: Jules Chéret (1838–1933), after studying colour lithography in London returned to Paris in 1866 and made Baron Haussmann's bleak 'new town' a city of posters and pretty 'Chérettes'. This petrol advertisement must date from before 1900, the year in which he retired from poster work to devote his energies to painting.

Abel Faivre (1867–1945) was at home in pastels as well as posters, being sometimes called the 'poor man's Renoir'. This publicity poster was for the Paris Salon in 1905.

pression of speed. Gaudy was probably the first artist to employ this device.

In fact the Salon commission for 1900 went to another Belgian, Privat Livemont, born at Schaerbeek in 1861, who had suddenly made his name at the age of 30 and never looked back. Livemont went in for remote blonde goddesses, beautifully drawn with tendrils of exotic foliage to embellish the allegory, but he also had a sharp eye for technical detail. In his 1902 Salon poster, for example, a vaguely Wagnerian goddess, lightly draped in muslin, poses in a cone of light from an overhead acetylene searchlight, at the wheel of a flower-strewn but unmistakeable De Dion (the Marquis de Dion was on the Salon's organizing committee) and the controls are technically correct. Livemont had much in common with Mucha, but while the latter's colours are jewelled, his are muted. One suspects that the shade of Privat Livemont has a hand in the design of present-day French banknotes, with their dim autumnal palette.

The A.C.F. Committee returned to Livemont for the 1903 Salon poster, but this time he gave them not a Frankish goddess on a mythologico-mechanical pedestal but a spring-like Botticellian maid in fashionable summery clothes

whom all the boys would dream about but few would venture to date. Again the colours are pale and muted. The work of Livemont and his contemporaries has been criticized for being more like an engraving than a poster. This is not really fair. At the turn of the century posters were studied as an art form, and avidly collected, either legitimately from dealers or clandestinely by following fly-posters at dawn armed with bucket and sponge. Specialist poster magazines were published both in Paris and London. What is more, the pace of life was much slower. Posters were inspected on foot, or from a slowly moving carriage. As cruising speeds grew, so advertising became bolder.

The Marquis de Dion, for one, moved away from Art Nouveau, and employed Misti, a draughtsman who could when he wished draw as boldly as his English contemporaries James Pryde and William Nicholson, who collaborated under the name of The Beggarstaffs. The girls in De Dion posters meanwhile ceased to be quite so pretty, so that the firm's host of feminine customers should not be antagonized. De Dions *voiturettes*, light to handle and easy to drive thanks to the expanding-clutches gearbox, were perfect 'ladies' cars', and were often smartly painted with vertical stripes or sham canework put on with the coachbuilder's equivalent of an icing-syringe. At this range it seems almost a pity that some of them were not decorated with flowers or arabesques, like a Peugeot ordered by the Bey of Tunis in 1894. Perhaps one had to be a North African potentate to afford such things.

There must have been good motoring talk in the Paris of those days, at the A.C.F. and at fashionable coachbuilders, who reckoned to receive their customers for drinks before luncheon, in the pubs near the factories and in the bistros where artists foregathered. The Natansons' literary magazine, *La Revue Blanche*, which ran from 1891 to 1903 became quite a motoring rendezvous, for the Natansons had a car, Tapié de Celeyran was a visitor, and Lautrec was there drawing illustrations and making his portrait of Mysia Natanson behind her pretty veil. There was Guillaume Apollinaire, the poet and critic who later established the theoretical basis of Cubism and rode many thousands of miles beside Francis Picabia, whose motoring seems to have been one long party during the high time of French motorcars before and after the Great War. Another contributor, Octave Mirbeau, later took motoring as his theme in a book

One of the few great painters to be interested in cars was Pierre Bonnard (1867–1947). One of the Revue Blanche *circle which included Forain and Toulouse-Lautrec, he drew this bold frontispiece for Octave Mirbeau's book somewhat later, in 1907. Facing page, top:* De Dion cars, *having an easy-change gearbox, were very popular with women drivers, at whom most of the firm's publicity was aimed. 'Misty' specialized in Gibson Girl heroines but this poster scarcely does him justice. Bottom:* This superb example of High Kitsch by Paul Gervais was exhibited at the Paris Salon de la Peinture *in 1904. It formed the frontispiece to Filson Young's* The Complete Motorist.

This 1894 Peugeot, made for the Bey of Tunis, must be one of the first examples of 'custom car' decoration.

of travels called, from the registration number of his 11 CV Renault, *La 628 E8*, and it was Pierre Bonnard who drew the illustrations, with a boldness that owed something to the Japanese prints on which he had modelled his posters for the *Revue Blanche* in the mid 1890s, and a humour all his own. Remembering later landscapes painted looking out through his studio window, one wonders whether it was gazing through the windscreen – or at least over the bonnet – of the 11 CV Renault that gave Bonnard a taste for this kind of composition. In fact the only painting made through a car windscreen which comes to mind is one dating from nearly a dozen years later, by Henri Matisse – the

Route de Villacoublay of 1917.

Some of the places which combined art with motoring were pretty rough. When the dealer Ambroise Vollard bought the entire output first of André Derain and then of Maurice Vlaminck, the two artists who had jointly invented Fauvism at Chatou, the pair of them came to Paris and were often to be found at the restaurant of the Père Azon, at the top of the Rue Ravignan. Just opposite were the studios of Picasso and Max Jacob, who always came in together, while other clients included Georges Braque and Guillaume Apollinaire the poet, critic and motorist. Apollinaire must often have talked cars with Kees Van Dongen and his gipsy girl friend, also with Derain and Vlaminck the ex-racing cyclist, when not hammering out Cubist theory – to Vlaminck's fury and disgust – with Braque and Picasso. The Père Azon gave everyone credit, Vlaminck tells us, and eventually went broke.

Many rude words went to and fro across the paper table-cloth no doubt at those meals on tick; and one of the rudest, if not the coarsest was 'pompier', the name given by 'proper', i.e., avant-garde artists, to slick, expensive Academicians, men like Henri Gervex, Henner and F. W. Bouguereau (1825–1903), whose canvases cost the rich bourgeoisie hundreds of thousands of francs. Occasionally but only occasionally some pompier would paint a motor car. This happened at the Salon of 1904, where customers could see a splendid bit of respectable nudery – 'art for tart's sake' – by a Bouguereau disciple named Paul Gervais, showing nymphs and satyrs disturbed at their revels by what was picturesquely known as a *teuf-teuf*.

Vlaminck would have laughed as loudly as any at this erotic flight of motoring fancy, but he might well have approved of another little painting on the walls of the same exhibition, by Marcel Clément, a windy street scene in Paris during winter in which the only vehicle, a Serpollet steam car, whispers past.

Illustrators there were in plenty, for in Edwardian times the weekly illustrated papers depended upon artists to illustrate the latest military revue, train wreck or motor accident: Moreaux and Vincent for example in France, Achille Beltrame in Italy, Caton Woodville and his colleagues at the *Illustrated London News* in London. But easel paintings of cars by themselves are rare. There may be many reasons for this. Automobile styles were evolving so fast that this year's car would look old-fashioned on next year's wall. The few avant-garde artists interested in motor car anatomy were apt to be bored with realistic painting, and, as many a painter will admit, cars are difficult to draw and as much a speciality as figure-painting, landscapes and marine work. So some marks for effort at least must be awarded to the American, John Sloan, a member of the so-called Trash Can school for his *Gray and Brass.* The passengers are almost cruelly life-like, like those Goya portraits of the Spanish royal family; the car seems to have got its proportions wrong somewhere, but it is a spirited piece and one of the rare U.S. works of its type.

The Sloan was painted in 1907, rather a significant year for our subject. This was the year of Octave Mirbeau's motoring travel book, *La 628 E8,* which was illustrated by Pierre Bonnard, and the year, too, in which Brooklands Motor Course, the world's first *ad hoc* car racing track was constructed at Byfleet, near Weybridge in Surrey. Before the opening the Napier concessionaire S. F. Edge, of Gordon Bennett fame, announced that he would back himself to average 60 miles an hour for 24 hours, an announcement received with incredulity by the press and dismay by tyre manufacturers. He did it, however, accompanied by two other big six-cylinder Napiers and the event was recorded for the London weekly *Graphic* magazine in a dramatic drawing of Edge's car seen head-on, headlamps blazing, during the night-time part of the run. The drawing is unsigned but may well be by Guy Lipscombe, whose slightly later oil painting of Tate's 60 horsepower Mercedes is on page 88. Lipscombe was more than a mere illustrator, a man like Abel Faivre the cartoonist, who produced acceptable pastels and has even been called the poor man's Renoir. Certainly neither of these two was a pompier.

Perhaps the king of the pompiers, where motoring was concerned, was Henri Gervex, whose *Dîner au Pré Catelan* not only appears in Maître Hervé Poulain's *L' Art et l'Automobile* but formed the jacket of *Academic Painters of the Nineteenth Century.* It shows the splendid new baroque restaurant which had recently been opened in the Bois de Boulogne from the outside looking in. Amongst the full-fig diners much of *le tout Paris* can be recognized: Santos Dumont, the airship and aeroplane pilot, the painter's wife, the Marquis de Dion and Mlle Liane de Pougy. In the background a diner's motor car drives away and a *chasseur* is beckoning for the next.

POPULAIRES 2 places 6cbx _ 4 places 8cbx de DION-BOUTON

1903   PUTEAUX (Seine)

45

Motoring Sport and Modern Art

Futurism to Dada via René Vincent

René Vincent (1879–1936) held one of the first driving licences. Architect by training, artist by inclination, he always got the technical details right. This sketch, from the Hervé Poulain collection, was the original for the Peugeot poster opposite.

NO PAINTING COULD TELL US MORE about the Edwardian motoring scene than the portrait of Max Pemberton (1863–1950), the British author of *The Amateur Motorist*, published in 1907. Max Pemberton was a journalist and popular novelist. He had been introduced to cars by a Benz in 1896 and a 6 hp Panhard the same year. The Panhard's reliability amazed him. 'I remember well my first ride in this little car and the astonishment which attended it. Why, there was no mutton-chop hunting whatever! Never once did the man get down and look for the meat in the cupboard.' After that he never looked back, and by the time his excellent book of advice appeared he owned a six-cylinder Hotchkiss, open, of course. 'For my part I would sooner take a train any day than drive a hundred miles in a stuffy limousine. Motoring loses its charm for me the moment I am boxed in. There is a sense of oppression in these closed cars which no amount of draughts – and draughts there are abundantly – can make good. The rattle of this class of car, the stuffiness of it, the limitations of it, are to me intolerable. I hear the laments of the lost complexion with indifference.' Those were the great days of the 'motor tour', when for the first time in fifty years, since in fact railways had ousted the post-chaise, it was possible to travel long distances, choosing one's route and stopping at will.

The English painter, Alfred Priest, has caught the mood brilliantly. Confident, expert, well-to-do, Pemberton stands beside his Hotchkiss, its paintwork and brass clean but not overdone. Priest certainly knew his craft; he was no pompier, but he could certainly handle all textures: the flesh, the long motoring coat, the sparkle of brass, the gleam of coachwork, the softness of the tyres contrasted with the metal lamps. Alfred Priest is an artist who deserves to be better known.

As a romantic and a sportsman Pemberton would have seen the bad poster advertising Brooklands (by Louis Vallet, b. 1856) and attended the opening of Brooklands during the year in which *The Amateur Motorist* came out. He had probably been to the Gordon-Bennett races with his friend and employer Lord Northcliffe (one of the earliest English car owners) and perhaps while visiting friends amongst the English colony in Florence or Bologna, watched the Coppa Florio races. Certainly he would have hated to miss the big race of 1906, the Grand Prix of the Automobile Club de France at Le Mans, which had superseded the Gordon Bennett series. Pressure of work may have kept him from taking part in the great Herkomer Tours (which we should call rallies) organized by the German-born society painter Sir Hubert Herkomer, which took their aristocratic and professional entrants over

Brooklands Track, opened in 1907, exerted a strong influence on motor car architecture. It bred 'wind-cheating' bodies of minimal frontal area, like the Vauxhalls designed by L. H. Pomeroy (above) in which the radiator was placed edge-ways to reduce drag, one of them being the first 3-litre to be timed at 100 mph. Right: Motoring portraits are very rare; this masterly painting of Sir Max Pemberton, author of The Amateur Motorist, *is by Alfred Priest.*

a large mileage of Continental and British roads during the past few seasons, but one cannot feel that he missed all three of the big races in 1907, that triple triumph for Felice Nazzaro, the great stylist from Fiat who won the Targa Florio in April with a 40 hp machine of 7.35 litres (125×150 mm bore and stroke), the Kaiserpreis on June 14th with a 60 hp, 8-litre machine (140×130 mm), and only a couple of weeks later the Grand Prix de l'A.C.F. with a 130 hp monster of 16.3 litres (180×160 mm). These were three excitingly diverse races, the first for allegedly non-racing cars through the mountains of Sicily, the second an 8-litre event for a trophy presented by the Kaiser, and the third a full-scale Grand Prix run on a limited-fuel basis over a long circuit at Dieppe. All the successful Fiats had four-cylinder side-valve engine and chain drive, but by this time many changes were taking place in car design: low-tension magnetos were giving place to H.T., shaft drive was beginning to supersede chains, the first straight-eight cylinder engines had appeared and Mercedes had already been using overhead camshafts for a couple of years.

Painting meanwhile was becoming rapidly more abstract, more difficult for outsiders to understand. One doubts whether the four-square Max Pemberton,

editor of *Vanity Fair* and ex-editor of the boys' magazine *Chums* would have found much in common with Matisse and Picasso, or with Derain who was in London at this time, painting bright Fauve works of the Pool of London and Westminster Bridge, the latter with cars driving on the right-hand side of the road.

While the Fauves were preoccupied with colour the Cubists were interested in

form, analyzing and synthesizing the shape of everyday objects, peering above and behind, seeking a new approach. In this study they were unconsciously joined by engineers and sporting drivers, many of whom were involved as designers or pilots with the study of aeronautics, where shape was of utmost importance. In 1907, with the opening of Brooklands racing track and aerodrome, airmen and car people had a centre for the exchange of ideas; and within a couple of seasons 'wind-cheating' had become an art in itself. The slim knifelike shape of L. H. Pomeroy's record-breaking Vauxhall named 'KN' was both scientific and sculptural; and it enabled the car to reach 100 miles an hour with what at the time seemed an impossibly small engine. Soon some of these lessons strayed from the race track to the design of sporting and competition road cars.

The big rallies which took the place of the Herkomer, the Tours instigated by the Kaiser's brother, Prince Henry of Prussia, brought forth Opel, Benz and Austro-Daimler cars every bit as outrageous to conservative minds as the exultant, subjective colours of Derain, Vlaminck and Matisse. 'Call those touring cars?' they cried, 'they're an outrage!', just as the Establishment was blowing through its whiskers at the Fauves and at Cubist paintings of Picasso, Gris and Braque. No Futurist Manifesto came from L. H. Pomeroy or Ferdinand Porsche to justify their Brooklands Vauxhall and Prince Henry Austro-Daimler, no engineering counterpart to the politico-philosophical proclamations of Marinetti despite an abundance of learned papers at the Institution of Automobile Engineers. Performance was its own justification, and went by the name of Progress, even though some examples of advanced engineering then and now may be difficult for the layman to 'read'.

An attempt to put the theory of Futurist painting into words was made by the painters Severini and Boccioni in their Manifesto of April 11th 1910, suggesting that form, space, movement, colour and sound were all inter-related. They could be seen as subjective and objective, artistic and technical. No doubt if the portrayal of movement in painting had been raised at dinner after an I.A.E. meeting Dr. F. W. Lanchester's table-napkin would have been covered with pencil sketches not unlike those of Balla; for having abandoned motor car design to his brother George, Dr. Fred Lanchester was now deep in three if not four dimensions, being concerned with the theory of aeronautics, where up,

This sculptural Austro-Daimler body was a successful pot-hunter designed by Dr. Ferdinand Porsche, conforming to Prince Henry Trial width-regulations only at the elbow line.

down, sideways and onward are inextricably intertwined and material progress always lags behind.

Futurist draughtsmen were very much bound up with the car. Artists at this time realized that a landscape viewed from a moving vehicle is essentially different from the same landscape seen statically. Different parts of it come into and out of focus, perspective changes continually, and by the fact of moving on one is able to see beyond and behind objects which to a static observer are merely two-dimensional. Passengers in a car can glimpse and they can gaze, while as speed rises and falls not only does perspective change but the amount of detail seen varies: one moment on a fast corner the only thing that exists is the tree the car seems about to hit; the next, having slowed, one sees violets by the roadside. In this way the motorist's world is quite alien from that of the walker. Not better nor worse, but different. Similar questions of time and space, the creation by the act of moving of a fourth dimension, not merely a sculptural third, had also preoccupied the Cubists, who were continually analyzing forms, opening up, flattening out, superimposing one viewpoint on another.

Automobiles of course were not the only miracle of the Futurist's age. Apart from the new flying machines there was the bioscope, alias cinematograph, which created moving pictures by taking a succession of stationary ones. The device built on the work of Eadweard Muybridge, the mid-Victorian photographer who by using multiple cameras taking a succession of stills against a calibrated background had made the first analysis of the way people and animals move. The French photographic firm of Gaumont evolved a primitive kind of speed-trap camera with a focal-plane shutter which had *two* slits in the blind, enabling successive images to be recorded on the same plate. With these images it was possible in theory at least,

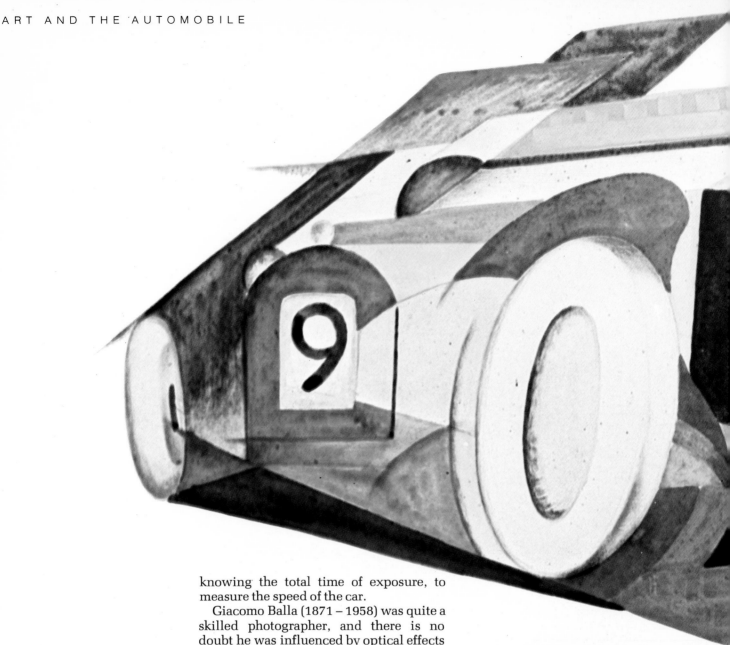

knowing the total time of exposure, to measure the speed of the car.

Giacomo Balla (1871 – 1958) was quite a skilled photographer, and there is no doubt he was influenced by optical effects of this sort. Balla would no doubt have adored the smoke swirling round wind-tunnel models of a later age, and the modern body-designer's technique of attaching tufts of wool to show the directions of airflow over different parts of the profile. Whether or not he was responsible for the English title of the painting in the Tate Gallery *(Wake of a Speeding Car)* I do not know, but both it and the Italian *Velocità astratta* – abstract speed – seem reasonably apt. Painters and aerodynamicists, unlike marine architects, have no visible displacement to guide them. Balla therefore made numerous experimental drawings and became so interested in speed that he sold all his previous output in 1912 when these had been going on for some months, and took to signing his work Futur Balla.

Gino Severini (1883–1966: Futurism seems to have conduced to long life) substituted brilliant Impressionist colours for Balla's muted tones, sometimes with echoes of Seurat's Pointillisme, sometimes in his own brand of Cubist Abstraction, as in his *Autobus* of 1912, while Luigi Russolo used the brightest Fauve colours during his own explorations of speed and sound and cars.

The dividing lines between Futurism and Vorticism are blurred: both schools shared an interest in the interpretation of movement. We can only imagine what Wyndham Lewis and Bomberg would have made of motor cars if they had tried, but good starting points for this exercise would be Marcel Duchamp's *Nude descending a Staircase* of 1912, and the study sent home from the Front by Henri Gaudier-Brzeska of a machine-gun in action. Did Lyonel Feininger ever paint motor cars as well as bicycle racers and motor cyclists? He certainly had the technique and style to suit it.

STEIGER-A.-G.
BURGRIEDEN-WTTBG.

Left: *Cubist, Futurist and Bauhaus influences are all apparent in this bold watercolour by M. L. Baugniet dated 1926, which is entitled* Etude de Vitesse en Course. *The artist, a Belgian, while eclectic in style, has been inspired by two compatriot marques, Minerva and Métallurgique. Above: Bauhaus sans-serif lettering and Teutonic brutality make this Steiger car advertisement by Engelhard typical of its time and place: Germany, circa 1925.*

remembered by the writer as *Le cheval vapeur*. This is now in the Musée de l'Art Moderne, Paris; it is very much in the spirit of Jacob Epstein's famous *Rock Drill* and of the bronze *Motorist's Head* by C. R. W. Nevinson, photos of which remain at the Tate although the original is lost. The Duchamp-Villon horse synthesized from imagined car-engines was probably seen as a knock at naturalistic pompier sculpture, but it also rather movingly looks forward to U.S. Pop Art of the 1960s and 1970s in which the idea of planned obsolescence is deliberately mocked. Pop Art quite often mocks motor cars and all that goes with them, while (Futurists apart) the Edwardian avant-garde largely ignored them. There is no Picasso or Braque car – and, for all his interest in cogwheels and levers no Fernand Léger car, although he did do an 'engine' painting. Machinery to Léger was no toy for the leisured classes but a road to prosperity and emancipation for the workers. He and Francis Picabia, whose Dada works come next in the story, had no sympathy for the high-flown vapourings of Marinetti and the Futurist manifestos, although they were quite at home with machines as such.

Concurrently with these experiments much down to earth work was being done. There was something of a gap during the pre-war years between the aesthetic probings of the avant-garde and the strict representations of *pompier* and illustrator. This territory came to be inhabited in Britain by painters inspired by Roger Fry's 'Post Impressionist' exhibition at the Grafton Gallery in October 1912 which, like the Armory show in New York a year later, introduced natives and painters alike to a whole new range of sensations. Here press and public met Fauves and Cubists for the first time and were outraged; and their outrage has lasted until the present day. Fry's doctrine that representation did not matter, only *form* being important and 'significant' form at that, not only had a liberating effect on painting in general by

The 'anti-Art' ideas of Marinetti, who proclaimed that the past was dead, museums should be thrown away and only the future was important, appealed not only to Futurists but to all the irreverent, witty, irascible irreconcilables who were painting in the fermentive years just before and during the outbreak of war – Wyndham Lewis, the larky Marcel Duchamp and his brothers Raymond Duchamp-Villon and Jacques Villon. Raymond Duchamp-Villon conceived one of the rare pieces of Vorticist sculpture in 1914, taking various elements suggested by the shape of conrods, cams and what may well be a rendering of Delage's desmodromic valve-gear, and blending them into a brilliantly organic yet mechanistic horse's head officially entitled *Le cheval majeur* but always

introducing new ideas to a territory in which Cézanne and Monet and van Gogh were (and still are sometimes) regarded as wild young men, but it also enabled artists who had hitherto been inhibited by the difficulty of getting a technical likeness to allow themselves the odd car or motor bus in their pictures.

Two such painters, neither of whom was strange to iconoclastic French aesthetes, since they had studied and lived in France, were Robert Bevan (1865–1925) and Charles Ginner (1878–1952) who was born at Cannes. Both men became members of the circle which became known as the Camden Town Group and both put motor vehicles in their compositions. Bevan's taxicabs (to be seen in paintings now at the Museum of London) look somewhat stilted – although not more so than the façades against which they stand – but Ginner attempted a much harder subject, in fact one almost proverbial in its complexity; the traffic at Piccadilly Circus.

He painted it not in a series of whorls as a Futurist would have done, nor naturalistically, but in a spirit of liberated realism which has pervaded so many English paintings since his day, for example Professor Carel Weight's *Wandsworth Stadium* of 1953.

The Ginner oil makes an interesting contrast with Gamy's *Place de l'Opéra*, a piece of commercial work probably commissioned by Renault. Captioned 'Renault 1913' and marked 'Mabileau & Cie, Editeurs Paris, copyright 1912', it is an evening scene on a chilly night, for the

women wear muffs and fur coats and the chauffeur of the elegant Renault *limousine de ville* is muffled against the cold, in contrast to his top-hatted passenger. The interest is in the motoring detail: the brass strips down the 'coal-scuttle' bonnet, the square 'opera' side-lamps on the pillars of the limousine, and the motor cabs in the background, shortly to become famous as the 'taxis of the Marne' which saved Paris from the Germans in 1914. This is good Gamy, nearly as successful as the best of the aviation scenes, and far far better than the rather summary motor racing prints of 1912–1914, which very seldom come off, although they were no doubt acceptable as showroom decoration.

By 1906 some charmingly delicate work was coming from the Montaut studios. Ernest Montaut himself had found a free watercolour style very suited to paintings which included airships as well as cars, especially in the almost ethereal *Raid Paris–Verdun*, recording the flight from Paris to Verdun by the airship *Ville de Paris* belonging to the great patron of aeronautics Henri Deutsch. These paintings too were no doubt advertising commissions, since the captions always contain names like Renault, Panhard, and Voisin Frères in connection with either the airframe or engines. Other, rather cruder publicity was undertaken for motor accessory firms like Lavalette-Eisemann, in which cars shaped like magnetos race melodramatically through mountain gorges, or the mountains themselves take on the form of magnetos, with appropriate electrical effects.

Perhaps even more persuasive than posters at this time were the evolving motor cars themselves which every year made headlines at the motor shows of London and Paris. Brooklands record-breakers and Prince Henry 'touring' cars had no impact upon the design of Grand Prix racers, which concentrated upon brute force,

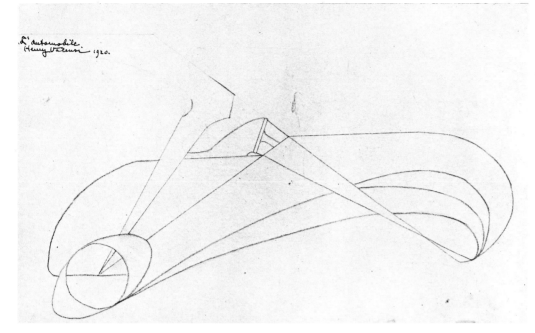

This Futurist drawing by Henry Valensi (1883–1960) was a study for an important and highly colourful oil. It may well have inspired the curvaceous coachwork of such makers as Saoutchik during the 1930s.

but they did open the minds of coachbuilder and public alike to the notion of motor cars as an art form, not merely a flight of steps, or an assemblage of seats or greenhouses, an elaboration of the horse-drawn carriage, but a new and rather chic shape.

There had always been a public for fast cars and smart, beautifully tailored interiors, but the moment when quick motoring became *snob* may well date from the day in 1912 when the Chevalier René de Knyff, pioneer racing driver, director of Panhard et Levassor and rowing man, went to Jean Henri Labourdette and said, 'Build me a car body like a skiff'.

When the coachbuilder explained that a carvel-built hull would be drastically weakened by doors, the Chevalier said, 'All right, no doors. People can step over the sides.'

'But the ladies?' queried Labourdette.

'They too. It is high time they showed us some leg.'

That was in 1912. The Chevalier's skiff body was built of copper-riveted natural mahogany strakes framed in ash, varnished to show the grain, and the wings were a work of art. Standing no higher than the low bonnet they seemed in Henri Labourdette's phrase to be flying alongside the car, and their form was quite as much sculpture as coachbuilding. Shaped rather like a mussel-shell from aluminium only 2 millimetres (.080 inches) thick, they were ribbed by hand like corduroy before being shaped. The painting too was entirely original. A coat of black was applied but wiped off before it was dry, so that the bare

metal showed on the ribs while the black remained in the hollows. A coat of transparent green lacquer was then brushed on over all, producing an iridescent effect which was as entirely new as the 'simultaneous' juxtaposition of bright colours by Robert and Sonia Terk Delaunay, which Guillaume Apollinaire christened Orphism. Between them the Chevalier and Labourdette started a fashion for boat-like open bodies which lasted well into the 1920s; the 1913 Salon was a riot of nautical fancy dress – cars in sailor suits – with bodies carvel or clinker built, lamps disguised as ships' ventilators and door-handles like rowlocks.

Although a few backwoodsmen were still buying *Roi des Belges* phaetons as late as 1912 and lamenting the lack of what they called 'beauty curves' in current models, fashion had moved swiftly on. Touring cars, originally open to all the winds that blew, quickly developed a 'scuttle dash' behind the bonnet to shelter the driver's feet, then his knees. The scuttle dash formed the foundation for a windscreen, and then 'half doors' were built between scuttle and front seats. These 'half doors' in front and the scarcely larger passenger doors behind grew higher until they were flush with the 'elbow line'. This happened first on competition cars, as we have seen. By 1908 not only Prince Henry Tour machines but ordinary open four-seaters were being delivered with high 'weather doors' in front hinged to a scuttle dash. Early efforts were clumsy but the 1907 Herkomer Tour car by Rothschild et Cie, the same maker's Racing Phaeton of 1908

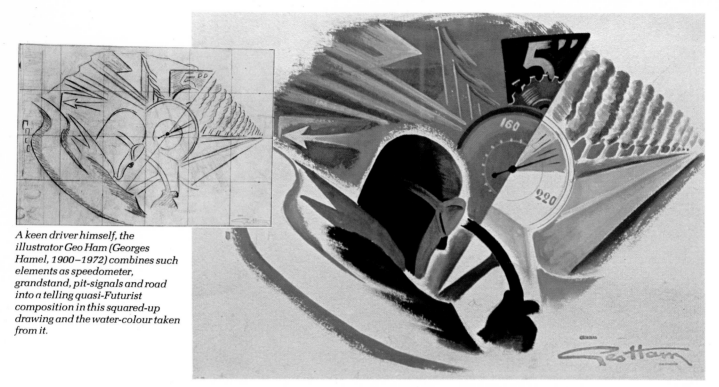

A keen driver himself, the illustrator Geo Ham (Georges Hamel, 1900–1972) combines such elements as speedometer, grandstand, pit-signals and road into a telling quasi-Futurist composition in this squared-up drawing and the water-colour taken from it.

and the Prince Henry cars which followed showed how a heightened bonnet could be arranged to blend with the scuttle and the latter could be integrated with the body to form a harmonious shape. Diehards spluttered, but it was soon obvious that flush-sided bodies were not only practical and good-looking in a modernistic way, but cheaper to make and repair. Closed cars too became less curly. Formal town carriages still smacked of the harness age, with chauffeur perched on what was still clearly a 'box' and usually without any door, but closed, flush-sided bodies for the owner driver were quite common by the outbreak of war.

A first-class example of the type is the big 40–50 horsepower Peugeot shown in a pair of 1915 prints by the leading motoring artist René Vincent, the first part of whose long career we should turn to now. Born in the same year as Ernest Montaut, René Vincent (1879 – 1936) was an artist and car enthusiast, having held one of the first driving licences in France. His elegant drawings spanned what we now call the Veteran, Edwardian, Vintage and Post-Vintage periods. His work illustrates perfectly the lasting love affair between *La France* and *l'automobile*.

Vincent was trained at the Institut des Beaux Arts as an architect, but he quickly turned to painting and became the best interpreter of motor cars in a social setting who ever lived because his fashion drawings, or rather his drawings of fashionable

women, were as good as his motor car work; it is no surprise to find that he worked for *La Vie Parisienne*. Henry Kistemecker turned to him for illustrations of his popular motoring novels – in sharp contrast to the British motoring romances of A. N. and C. M. Williamson, which relied on rather smudgy photographs – and the motor industry sought him out. One of the most coveted bits of motoring ephemera is the catalogue Vincent did for Berliet in 1906, showing the success of Berliet cars in various big cities round the world. The settings are rather trite, but probably just what the client wanted: with snake-charmer in Bombay, outside a beer-garden in Nuremberg and with an Indian brave, camp-fire and black chauffeur typifying Chicago. London has a hansom cab beside the Berliet brewer's dray and the Seville scene has a tall *limousine de voyage* impeded by bulls while its owners reason with a mounted *vaquero*. Naturally Vincent feels most at home in Paris at the races. This is 1906 so the lady owner of a winning horse is seated in a motor Victoria, chauffeur and footman on the 'box' while the jockey recounts the story of the race. As always with René Vincent the Gainsborough hat and parasol, the car's brakedrums and the party of well-dressed well-wishers are all equally well handled, while a few details, realistically drawn but incomplete – in this picture a table-top with champagne and part of two chairs – help to set the scene and give depth to the

Prominent in the Mabileau lithographic studio after the death of Ernest Montaut, who was the senior partner, Gamy painted in many styles, the most delicate of which was reserved for aeronautical subjects. This realistic illustration of a Renault in the Place de l'Opéra dates from 1912.

composition. Thanks no doubt to his architectural training Vincent can indicate a complete garage by means of two cracks in the concrete and part of a roof-truss. This talent proved useful in those booklets which took the customer on a trip round the Berliet factory: the interest is concentrated where it is wanted – on a pillar drill or whatever – but always there are figures to lend interest and some detail providing location and perspective.

From Berliet Vincent moved to Peugeot, once again with humorous drawings, some dated 1908. He was to return to them later. In 1912 Peugeot made cars of all sizes from the *Bébé* designed by Bugatti to a majestic 40–50 horsepower 8-litre. They also won the French Grand Prix with the first of Ernest Henri's twin-overhead-camshaft engines, playing David to Fiat's Goliath and bringing the age of monster racing-cars to an end. Peugeot had plenty to say and René Vincent said it for them well. They pioneered front-wheel brakes in the 1914 French Grand Prix which they lost after a tremendous duel with Mercedes; but Peugeot racing cars went on to Indianapolis, for the 500 Miles track race, which they won in 1916 and 1919. Perhaps it was one of these races which Vincent's poster was advertising with the slogan *'L'Industrie française triomphe dans le monde grâce à Peugeot'*. The viewpoint – car seen almost head-on as though by an observer by the roadside – had by this time become rather a cliché, having been used twice already in Peugeot advertising by Ernest Montaut's Gamy, but the highlights on bonnet and wheel-spokes and the mechanical detail, rendered faithfully but unobtrusively even though the axle is leaping up and down, is very Vincent. He was a good dramatist as well as a fine

draughtsman, for as the front wheels bounce clear of the road the whole car seems to be driving at the observer. The canted axle, spinning tyres and Peugeot radiator dominate the picture and it is only after examining it for some time that one realizes that the driver, almost hidden behind the scuttle, and the rear wheel in its cloud of dust are impossibly far away. Here René Vincent's eye is a wide-angle lens.

Whatever circuit the stylized background is supposed to represent – and the landscape is hidden by dust-clouds which are there to silhouette the lines of the car, not conceal bits of machinery – the Peugeot must be dated after 1914 because Vincent shows it with front-wheel brakes and it was not until that famous Grand Prix at Lyons that Peugeot pioneered these for racing. It is a safe bet anyway that this poster dates from the war or just afterwards, since within a couple of weeks of Lyons the nations which had produced Peugeot and Mercedes, Boillot and Lautenschlager, had taken up arms against one another. Four weeks later, from September 6th–19th 1914 came General von Kluck's advance on Paris which was halted by the Battle of the Marne. Somewhere there must be an oil-painting in the grand manner of the famous little twin-cylinder Renault taxis chuffing their way from Paris to the battlefield laden with troops, although admittedly a cab has hardly the panache of a charger. Certainly the illustrators worked pretty hard on the theme and the *Taxis de la Marne* have passed into motoring folklore.

In his *Ambusqué* gouaches painted in 1915 René Vincent perfectly captures the mood, a mixture of cynicism and heroics that the French always manage so well. There had been much talk of rich young

Le départ de l'Ambusqué

Le retour de l'Ambusqué

René Vincent, who worked for La Vie Parisienne, L'Illustration *and other Paris magazines was equally at home with fashion and cars. The point of this 1915 diptych joke is explained in the text. Note the economy with which Vincent indicates a garage setting.*

men 'dodging the column', or, in the language of a later war, 'keeping away from the sharp end' by the help of friends in high places. So Vincent takes a sly look at the smart young officer off to a comfortable war in his 8-litre Peugeot *conduite intérieure* with his race glasses, hat-box, hipbath, tantalus and coffee-grinder. Languidly he kisses his mother's hand while footmen are loading the car and his valet, self-conscious in uniform, is getting nowhere with the *soubrette*. A classic picture of an *Ambusqué*, which meant someone safely sheltered from the firing line. But

now for a little touch of heroism.

Our warriors drive into a German ambush: they become *embusqués* in the original meaning of the word. The Uhlans are routed, their spiked helmets and carbines captured. Picturesque wounds are received by warriors and Peugeot alike (note the bandage round a front tyre), civilian gear is forgotten, and all return to a hero's welcome, not least the valet, received warmly behind the car. All very much in the spirit of *La Vie Parisienne,* enormously René Vincent, who gives us motor cars, exquisite uniforms, elegant women, some sly touches and a trace of sentiment. Vincent shared Jules Chéret's liking for laughter and girls. He continued drawing painting and poster work into the 1920s and 1930s, and so we shall be meeting his work again in a later chapter.

A wanderer through wartime France during the First World War might not have found many easel paintings of cars, but he could have found at least one, for in 1917 Henri Matisse (1869–1954) painted *La Route de Villacoublay* seen from the back seat of a closed and somewhat elderly car through the upright windscreen and side windows, the latter with straps to open and close them like those in old railway carriages. The screen pillars break up what might otherwise be an uneventful bit of tree-lined road, just as the studio windows concentrate the view in many a Bonnard. The interest so far as we are concerned in this otherwise classic Matisse lies in the foreground. The car has a scuttle dash, beyond which can be seen the tops of brass lamps; but no instruments come into the picture, being hidden by the back of the driver's seat. There is no passenger seat to be seen, possibly because this *conduite intérieure* body was one of those built with a single entrance on the passenger's side like the front door of a house, with a corridor stretching from dashboard to back seat. This was done quite often between 1910 and 1914 when towering millinery made cars very high and more than one door would have seriously weakened the structure. This car, like almost all high-quality French cars until the 1930s, has right-hand drive despite a right-hand rule of the road. Is it philistine to speculate as to the make of car, given that the steering-wheel has a very thick wooden rim and five wide tapering (and no doubt cast aluminium) spokes? Matisse would have been forty-eight when this canvas was painted in 1917 and had been turned down for military service. He moved to Nice to live the same year.

As a contrast to the elaborate pieces, the absence of which from the War Museum is such a solace, we have the wartime output of the neutrals and expatriates. These did *not* include Guillaume Apollinaire who, naturalized French only in 1913, joined the army and was to die of his wounds in 1918. Francis, Picabia on the other hand, who had driven so many miles in peacetime at high speed with Apollinaire by his side, shared the modern view that wars are noisy and dangerous, no place for the eager hedonist; besides, he was Cuban by birth. By pulling strings – 'wangling' was the contemporary word – he was made chauffeur to a general, which kept him out of the trenches, and in 1915 he was sent with a trade mission to Cuba. On his way back he succeeded in getting stuck in New York City.

Once in New York he naturally looked up his old friend of 1913, Alfred Stieglitz, at the Little Gallery of the Photo-Secession at 291 Fifth Avenue where since 1907 Stieglitz and Edward Steichen had fostered modern art as much as photography, and introduced New York to the School of Paris. Along with Bernard Shaw, Maurice Maeterlinck and Gertrude Stein, Picabia had been one of the contributors to their magazine *Camera Work*, which published fine reproductions and articles on painting as well as photography – work in any medium, Stieglitz explained, which showed 'honesty of aim, honesty of self-expression, honesty of revolt against the autocracy of convention'. In 1917 American newspapers were still purple in the face over the Armory Show, the International Exhibition of Modern Art organized by Stieglitz in March 1913. *Chez* Stieglitz, Francis Picabia found a haven of revolt. Marcel Duchamp turned up also in 1915, so Dada, which is the French for 'hobby horse' in both literal and metaphorical meanings and so an appropriate name for the zany anarchisms of Picabia and Duchamp, was well represented.

Motor cars and mockery were never far from Picabia's mind. With Alfred Stieglitz he helped launch an avant-garde magazine called *291* from the address on Fifth Avenue, and to it contributed characteristic drawings. '*Ici, c'est ici Stieglitz*' is stencilled on one of these, and, below, the words '*Foi et Amour*', also stencilled; above in flowery black letter capitals is IDEAL. An elegant, mocking abstract, the design boldly features a vest-pocket Kodak – a gentle jibe at Stieglitz the professional – its bellows detached, forming a ramp or staircase leading perhaps to the attic of-

fices of *291*; and behind this photographic detritus Picabia has sketched, in the careful style of an engineer's blue-print, the handbrake and gear-levers of a car. Mocking and shocking the American worship of machines, he built automobile bits into drawings like the provocatively titled *Young American Girl in a State of Nudity* who is partly sparking-plug, and a self-portrait which is mainly a klaxon horn.

Soon, brought low by over-living, Picabia sent for the girl friend Gabrielle Buffet, who had pulled the strings to keep him out of the war, and married her in New York. The marriage did not last long but Picabia recovered and it was fun while it lasted. His homage to Gabrielle as an open double-hinged two-piece windscreen is a charming frolic, elegant like all his work, brilliantly composed and charged with linear and sexual ambiguities.

Picabia was a master of the visual pun, the echoes and cross-references which the cartoons of Walt Disney taught everyone to see and enjoy. His work is epigramatic, full of 'in' jokes; nothing could be further removed from the art of the illustrator, and yet when the war finished and it was once more possible for *grands routiers* to drive at high speed over the neglected shell-pocked macadam and *pavé* roads of France, Francis Picabia and René Vincent, both now forty and prosperous, had at least two interests in common: smart women and fast cars. The story is told that one day while motoring near Cannes Picabia came upon a country wedding, stopped and joined in the celebrations. He was last seen disappearing into the distance with the bride in his white Mercedes.

Bonnard and Matisse (1869–1954) were two Impressionists who tackled car subjects. The composition above of a road seen through a car windscreen – La Route de Villacoublay – strongly suggests Bonnard but is in fact by Matisse.

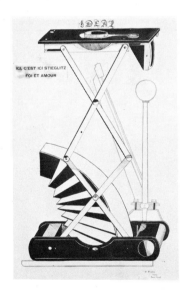

Visiting his New York photographer friend Alfred Stieglitz in 1915, the larky Francis Picabia combines elements from car and camera to suggest the attic art gallery at 291 Fifth Avenue.

Cars of the Jazz Age

Styling, coachwork and interior appointments

King Alfonso of Spain was a great car enthusiast. He allowed his name to be associated with one of the world's first sports cars, the Hispano-Suiza 'Alphonse XIII' model, current during the period 1912–14. René Vincent perfectly captures the atmosphere with these catalogue illustrations showing a short-chassis two-seater and (facing page) a formal closed car with single offside door giving access to the owners' accommodation.

THE FRENCH MOTOR INDUSTRY got swiftly off the mark after the war. By autumn 1919 they were ready with a full-dress Salon in the Grand Palais. Old names from the great days were there, Renault, Mors, Brasier, Panhard, Peugeot . . . and makers of aeroplanes had joined in, making a bid for the carriage trade: Farman, builders of trainers

and bombers, and Avions Voisin, whose bombing aeroplanes, heavy but strong, had pioneered steel construction and oleopneumatic suspension. The French 'ace of aces' René Fonck, top-scoring fighter pilot of the Allied air forces, also tried his hand at large luxury cars, although his company lasted little more than a year. Undeniably, though, the finest car in the show was Marc Birkigt's latest design, the six-cylinder H6 Hispano-Suiza. This was the make which in René Vincent's splendid pre-war catalogue had quite justifiably proclaimed itself *'La Reine de la Route'*; and the new model might well have been called *'L'Impératrice'* except that it needed no fancy labels to make its point. Technically it was the most advanced car in the world. The largely aluminium engine was based on the firm's 200 horsepower V-eight which had been used in thousands of British and French single-seaters during the war including the SPADs flown by Guynemer and the famous Stork squadron, the Escadrille des Cigognes. The brakes not only operated on all four wheels – which very few did at that time – but were also servo-assisted like all the best braking-systems today. As if that were not enough the tall radiator was one of the most imposing ever designed; and above the winged enamel Hispano badge the cap carried a flying stork mascot, recalling l'Escadrille des Cigognes. This mascot was

Eve and her Car

Also by René Vincent is this drawing of 'Eve' and her front-braked Delage. Below: This economical line drawing by J. A. Mercier, dated 1929, captures the sophisticated elegance of the age. On the facing page, the upper picture illustrates one of René Vincent's own short stories in L'Illustration. The boy is saying 'Go on mother, put your foot down and get past that Packard!' Below: This sketch for a Citroën poster was made by the French artist A. E. Marty (born 1882). Note the masterly way in which the curve of the eyebrows is echoed by the steering-wheel, quarter-light, headlamps and chevron trademark.

one of the two most famous mascots of all time, the other being Charles Sykes's Spirit of Ecstasy for Rolls-Royce. It was designed by a member of the Hispano-Suiza company, Louis Massuger, who had driven their cars in competition before the war and stayed on to become field service manager on the aviation side throughout the 1930s. Production mascots bear the signature of François Bazin, whose name appears on a number of French radiator emblems.

Unlike the side-valve Rolls-Royce, its principal rival, the Hispano engine was tall. This in itself would have called for a fairly high bonnet; but there was another reason no doubt: Marc Birkigt was identifying his car with the S.E.5 and SPAD single-seater fighters which had had car-type radiators and were the most powerful and exciting machines that the ordinary public was familiar with. A high bonnet entailed high sides and therefore a clean horizontal line from radiator to poop. No wonder that the great Paris coachbuilders like Chapron, Kellner, Letourneur et Marchand and Labourdette competed for delivery of Hispano-Suiza chassis. The important thing was to get started, to satisfy the clamour for freedom and mobility as customers emerged from wartime restraint.

Although the extremes in body design did not range all the way from pompier to Dada as they now did in painting, coachbuilders found plenty of room for self-expression. One body by Belvalette on a Renault was as pompier as Meissonier himself, for in style it harked back to the *dormeuse* or travelling carriage of the eighteenth century, and was hung by straps from C-shaped springs like a Lord Mayor's coach, its Louis XV interior done out in dark blue cloth, with quilted roof-lining and quarters. Yet the chassis had modern wire wheels and there was a high door to the chauffeur's compartment that was almost ahead of its time. Elsewhere though, the tentative beginnings of Art Déco were beginning to emerge. Gabriel Voisin, whose memoirs tell more about his love life than his machines, led the way with a light-weight competition closed car that looked like a cabin biplane without wings, all straight lines and angles, the sides slanting inwards above the waistline and the waist higher than usual, approximating to the proportions of the Golden Section. And as a sporting car it could have quite a low roof because the occupants would be cloth-capped or bare-headed. Gabriel Voisin had already caught the mood and set a fashion. Straight lines in bodywork went well with the clothes of the Tubular Twenties. Suddenly after the war motoring moved up in the world. It became smart, part of what Parisians at the time called *'le high-life'*. Fashionable families ran two cars at least, an open fronted Brougham or coupé de ville for town and theatre work, and an open four-seater Torpedo. Perhaps even two Torpedoes, one *classique* with high sides and big windscreens, the other *grand sport*, with minimal mudguards windscreens and doors, for the enjoyment of speed and fresh air.

During 1920 French coachbuilders excelled themselves and the fashion papers took motor cars seriously. The first issue to come from the newly opened Paris offices of *Vogue* had a motor car and model girl on the cover. The motoring paper *L'Auto* brought things home to Parisians by holding a concours d'élégance at Bagatelle, in the Bois de Boulogne during the following summer, and no one could say whether the closed cars or the open ones were the more fun. Some of the wittiest designs came from Henri Labourdette, who showed a coupé de ville with V windscreen like the sports cars of the time and made the division behind the open-air chauffeur V-shaped to match. He called it a *Limousine en coupe-vent*. Another of his creations was a *skiff-cab*, an open body with walnut and mahogany decking like a motor boat, but with a tiny closed compartment right aft, just like a hansom cab. These great Hispano, Renault and Delage creations were as frivolous as women's hats, and the great coachbuilders, like the fashion houses, brought out 'collections' making sure that the line changed every year. One could no more appear at Biarritz or Deauville in last year's Hispano than in last year's fur coat or wearing last year's breed of dog.

The sad thing is that women who bought cars like this, Mademoiselle Suzanne Deutsch de la Meurthe, the Dolly Sisters, Mistinguett, do not seem to have included them in portraits painted by artists in vogue, Kees van Dongen, for instance, or Marie Laurencin. It is understandable. Concours d'élégance – for ensemble of lady and car – were covered photographically for the illustrated papers, and who would wish to be identified forever with a 1923 car? For an idea of what might have been we must turn to posters and catalogues, where René Vincent shone as brightly as ever, producing his sure-fire amalgam of women + fashion + car, making certain in this way that all readers, of both sexes, had a reason for a long, covetous study. Salmson knew their business when they brought out the 'new 10 hp' motor car stripped for action, with a damn-your-eyes blonde dressed to kill; it was a certainty that either would be a real handful, and that one might get you the other. This drawing is vintage Vincent in every sense, more taut and sophisticated than the humorous pre-war drawings, not pretty and sentimental as he afterwards became.

Meanwhile if easel painters were under-employed by the motoring world, coach-painters were at a premium. The Edwardian fashion for basket-work finishes was revived in the 1920s. Split cane was no longer used. Instead a mixture of white lead, whiting, shellac, gold-size, turpentine and pigment could be bought from a firm named Leblanc in the rue de Valois,

This front cover for Vogue *of November 1st 1924 was painted by Georges Lepape (1887–1971) and entitled* Robe optique assortie à la carrosserie. *The 'optical' dress and the Voisin colour scheme were designed by Sonia Terk Delaunay, wife of Robert Delaunay the Orphist painter. Stripes, checks, lozenges and tartans were popular for cars at this time. Sonia Delaunay, born 1885 and still working when this was written, was one of the founders of Op Art, a precursor of Vasarely.*

Paris, and squeezed on out of the tube; like icing a cake. The fashion of 1919–1920 was for dark caning against a light ground, the most popular post-war colours for cars as well as clothes being the lighter shades of grey and biscuit, which led a Londoner to remark 'French spaniels no longer fawn – they beige'.

Basketwork panelling generated other ideas. Colour schemes in 1922 were original and startling. A Sizaire-Berwick car at the Salon had its lower panels overpainted with a lozenge motif, while Gabriel Voisin, never knowingly out-done, showed an angular four-light saloon *à l'écossaise*, inventing a tartan of his own

design built up from two criss-crossing shades of grey which started a fashion and kept one particular coach-painter busy for several seasons. Paris was the centre of fashion, and of the luxury trades. Designers let themselves go inside the car as well as out, decorating cars as they would the interior of a fashionable flat. Instead of plain leather or broadcloth they used fabrics with stripes or checks, or various brocades and even figured plush. As a change from beige, cars might be dazzlingly bright: dark blue or green fine-lined in carmine or gold, or sham caned in black on panels of red, orange or ivory. A Panhard by Kellner the coachbuilder in crimson

*Another period piece by
A. E. Marty, dating from 1927–28,
when skirts had just risen to the
knee and petrol was still sold in
cans.*

lake ('Panhard red') was sham-caned in gold. The gold-rush continued into 1923. Everywhere car panels were fine-lined, criss-crossed, basketed and betartanned, although even this was not the summit, as we shall see.

For a year or two in the early-1920s, during the run-up to the Exposition des Arts Décoratifs of 1925 and for a few seasons afterwards, motor cars enjoyed an artistic life of their own. Not only as fashion accessories (although this in itself was something new) but as works of art in their own right, like the Voisin in Georges Lepape's front cover for *Vogue*. Nothing could be more stylish nor more in the spirit of the time than the Jazz Age patterns on the dress and matching car, nor the attitude of the girl herself. 'By 1924', we are reminded by Mr. James Laver, 'the tubular look had established itself. The figures in fashion plates grew taller and thinner until they were, in proportion to the rest of the body, almost twice the natural height of any living woman. The Rubenesque ideal was gone, even Botticelli was discredited; El Greco reigned supreme.' Lepape's girl

looks down on the rest of creation from a great height; she has cropped her hair to fit under a cloche hat or linen flying-helmet and achieved the 'slim boyish figure' which was every girl's current ideal, and which was to bring with it a boy's freedom of movement and behaviour. We know that the designer of the dress material, and of the pattern on the probably fabric body of the car was Sonia Delaunay (born 1885 and still painting in 1978) who had married Robert Delaunay (1885 – 1941) in 1910. Together the Delaunays brought bright *fauve* colours into Cubist painting. Apollinaire chose to see musical analogies in their work, which he therefore called Orphism (from Orpheus). Sonia Delaunay's palette and geometrical arrangments can now be seen as fore-runners of Op Art, as they seem to anticipate Vasarely. Within a year of this drawing (dated November 1st 1924) an even greater revolution was to take place. Hemlines rose from ankle to knee and for the first time in the history of fashion civilized women exposed their legs.

The architects of the New Woman were

The 'dazzle painting' used by the Royal Navy to confuse the enemy as to the size, type and direction of vessels had its origins in Cubist painting. Here, anticipating Salon fashions of some years later, is the Straker-Squire of H. Kensington-Moir, an ex-naval officer, on Brooklands in about 1921.

It seems odd that coachbuilders and their fashionable clientèle did not borrow the idea of 'dazzle painting' from the ships of the Great War when Cubist – or perhaps more properly Vorticist – designs in contrasting patches were painted over the hull and superstructure, making it difficult for enemy vessels, especially submarines, to recognize them. By breaking up the outline the designs also acted as camouflage and made it difficult to estimate size, speed and direction of travel. A dazzle-painted Hispano-Suiza might have caused delightful confusion outside Maxim's or on the sea-front at Deauville, but the only example of a dazzle-painted car on record is a Straker-Squire raced at Brooklands during the early 1920s by H. Kensington-Moir, later team manager to Bentley Motors. There was no mistaking Bertie Moir's car.

There is a good story about a character who was around in Paris during the 1920s. This was Dominique Lamberjack, one of those Bugattistes who had petrol in his

dress designers: Jean Patou, Lanvin, Molyneux, Piguet, Lelong and two women, Chanel and Schiaparelli who in the long run probably proved more influential than any, not only in the special world of fashion but in wider fields of design.

Through Chanel and Schiaparelli the ideas of men like Picasso, Jean Cocteau and Léger filtered via haute couture into the surrounding world of furniture, jewelry and cars.

No artist could be more faithful to the period than Marcel Hemjic in these two drawings of motorists and their dogs, the girl with a V windscreen, the man with the fold-flat type.

The cloth cap from which Zyg Brunner's drawing – La casquette à damier, circa 1928 – takes its title perfectly complements the cloche hat. This economical draughtsman was especially popular in the United States.

veins. He had raced motor cycles, established various speed records at Montlhéry with motor cycles and cars, and was a leading rally driver of his day. He also held a Bugatti agency, and made astonishing speeds on the road.

When it came to painting his latest closed Bug., he decided to have some fun. The roof and rear trunk would be black as was universal for coupé and saloon in those days, but one side of the car was to be black, the other side red. The coachbuilder raised his eyebrows, and so Lamberjack explained.

'Look', he said, 'I'm fed up with these Boy Racers who think they're God's gift. It's time someone taught them a lesson. So the right side of my car will be red, and the left side will be black. I shall be driving along and one of these sham Chirons will start a dust-up. After a couple of kilometers I shall let him "win" and he'll overtake a black Bugatti. When he loses me from his mirror he will eventually slow down. Then I shall turn on the heat, and he will see a red Bug. overtake and disappear into the distance. This will make him mad. He'll do everything he knows to catch the red car again and once out of sight I shall slow to a sedate pace and he'll hardly notice the black car trundling gently along, being intent on catching the red one... With luck he will burst his engine or go into the ditch; if not there will soon be a black car on his heels and he just won't know where he's at. And a good riddance of bad rubbish. It might even teach him to drive!'

Here was a joke that Duchamp and Picabia would have appreciated: a blend of trompe l'oeil and Dada, with a hint of the Surrealism that was to come.

While cars remained outside the main artistic current during the 1920s except as works of art in their own right, because the major painters were concerned with subjective exploration of mainly indoor themes, they did find their way occasionally into the work of masters like Raoul Dufy, Kees van Dongen and Marie Laurencin whose frivolous decorations were very much in the taste of the time. Unfortunately Raoul Dufy always keeps his distance from the scene; not that that is in itself a disadvantage for he provides splendid panoramas of the sporting world, taking us to Longchamp, to Deauville and into apartments where Cocteau and Stravinsky may have bandied arguments with Le Corbusier and his friend Gabriel Voisin on questions of form and draughtmanship and of the nature of the machine. Dufy's work has come to seem almost documentary: the frothiest of documentaries it is true (after his more serious Fauve and Cubist beginnings), poised somewhat perilously upon the edge of art and decoration, but as Parisian as Marcel Proust. Every buyer of Dufy's feathery confections would have owned a Ballot, Hispano or Delage, or perhaps Renault 40 torpedo like those drawn by Marcelle Pichon. Their playmates would have been the people in A. E. Marty's cool, elegant posters, the *jeunesse folle* clambering expressively into a Type 43 Bugatti outside the Dôme for Jean-Emile Laboureur to capture in one of his etchings. These were the 'Bright Young Things' and the 'lost generation' one meets in the early works of Aldous Huxley and Evelyn Waugh. They and their cars have been perfectly captured not only by René Vincent (inevitably) but by J. A. Mercier whose crisp line drawings illustrate Pierre Benoit's novel *L'Auto* (1929). Bonamoni captured the same feeling in his Art Deco designs which suggest without

actually stating that the cloche-hatted heroine has a rendezvous – misplaced no doubt – with the poor man cast as a playboy in Pierre Frondaye's *L'Homme à l'Hispano* (*circa* 1922). Nothing could have been livelier at this time than the American artist Zyg Brunner, whose drawings straddled the Atlantic and should have been the subject of an auction between Arlen, Coward, Evelyn Waugh, Aldous Huxley and F. Scott Fitzgerald, the

spoils to be shared between all bidders. These pictures are a reminder that motoring was as much a part of the fashionable scene as horse-racing and the casino.

For the developing shape of cars the man ultimately responsible was an ex-airman named Charles Torrens Weymann, whose aeroplane factories remained full of material after the end of the war, demanding some profitable outlet. Weymann decided that the lessons learned in aeroplane work

A cover for L'Illustration (October 6th 1934), this A. E. Marty watercolour is called 'Let's take the car' – in this case a fashionable but ambiguous vehicle with elements from several makes, including the new traction avant Citroën sold in Britain as the Super Modern Twelve.

could be used in making lightweight closed cars, and set about producing a car body consisting of a flexible lightweight skeleton covered in waterproof fabric stretched tight. This body could be driven fast over bad roads without hammering itself to pieces and, since the joints were padded, without the rattles inseparable from closed bodywork until then. What is more the speed and economy with which bodies could be built was a revelation to the industry. A Weymann body by-passed the sheet-metal and paint shops completely. No panel-bashing. No filling, priming, rubbing down wet-and-dry; no undercoats top coat and varnishing with lengthy delays between each: simply a roll of fabric to be cut and attached as required. No paint-work to craze, no varnish to dull.

Textured fabrics added a new dimension – hessian, morocco, crocodile. Fancy finishes were no problem: just choose a

Fabric bodies, consisting of imitation leather stretched over an articulated wooden frame, were introduced by C. T. Weymann soon after the First World War and were widely copied, since they bypassed the manufacturing bottlenecks of panelbeaters and paint shop. The car shown is a well-restored 20 hp Rolls Royce of about 1928.

fancy fabric. One of the first to realize this was the London coachbuilder, Windover, who showed a Minerva with the lower panels done in black and white check.

C. T. Weymann enabled body design to progress. He provided techniques on which artist and designer could build. The first fabric saloons were square, boxy and dull copies of coachbuilt saloons. It will be remembered that big closed cars before and after the war, like the one Matisse drew on the Villacoublay road, had only one door, and that narrow to avoid weakening the structure and straining the hinges. With Weymann lightweight methods of construction and cross-tensioning wide doors were no problem. Suddenly close-coupled coupés became possible, with all passengers seated within the wheelbase. Untroubled by weight he built bodies wider, over the wheel arches; and inevitably, the *Zeitgeist* working as it does, the straight-up-and-down tubular look of women's clothes was reflected in motor car design. At the 1924 Salon Gabriel Voisin, most Parisian of car men, showed a fabric-covered plywood body with wide doors hung on piano hinges and the sides running down flush to the running board. In this he was in fact following a lead set by Lancia on their astonishing independently-sprung Lambda model launched the previous year. The Lambda, fitted with detachable hard top and painted orange shading into carmine, received no praise for its low build and good visibility, only criticism for having foot wells each side of the propeller-shaft tunnel. Nobody seemed to notice – except Gabriel Voisin – the neat body sides dropping sheer to the running board.

Weymann arithmetic affected design in other directions. Fabric is far lighter than glass, so it was logical in fabric bodies to raise the waistline as women had raised their skirts. Within a few seasons windscreens were like letter-box slots on both fabric and coachbuilt bodies.

Artistically cars blossomed in 1924 and 1925. It was a time not only of fabric but of colourful coachbuilt bodies, when young bloods were bent on beating the Paris-Deauville and Paris-Nice unofficial records. People still talked of the strange tank-like cars raced by Bugatti and Voisin in 1923, and for the passively sporting family there was a host of exciting semi-sports touring cars with a nautical or at least seaside tang. Their sides were now higher to keep out the rigours of the elements, but they were still decked like boats, with planking in mahogany or walnut or with ash decks and framing. Many of these big touring cars had a sort of half-deck amidships carrying a windscreen for the people in the back. These folding screens were called *tabatières* or *boucliers* in France, while the same style of body in the United States was called a twin-cowl phaeton. Several coachbuilders enclosed the rear-seat passengers altogether in a sort of hansom cab perched over the axle. V windscreens, one of the prettiest fashions of the 1920s were very much in fashion.

Inside, wood veneers were all the rage, as they were on contemporary furniture. Mahogany and walnut were contrasted with lighter woods, such as harewood (sycamore), holly and satinwood. Ebony cross-banding and stringing were to be seen. Inlaid lines became popular as decoration for interior cabinetwork, and Labourdette, for one, used lacquer by Dunand as a change from polished woodwork. At the same time he introduced another famous Art Deco name when he relieved the plainness of the division by means of frosted Lalique glass plaques, lit from behind. Boat bodies were everywhere, and even their decks were sometimes inlaid with marquetry effects, never mind the sun and the rain. Long, rakish wings were the fashion, sometimes with slatted running boards, sometimes with only a step; front dumb-irons were valanced, tidying the front-end view, while, to restore the balance, fancy-dress sporting bric-a-brac was added wherever possible, in the form of tool- and battery-boxes, bedizened with nickled hinges and locks. A large nickel-plated swivelling spotlight often completed the effect, suggesting that their owner was a *grand routier*, driving far and fast by night; this was often mere fancy dress. Serious fast drivers preferred to shed weight rather than add it, and probably owned a Bugatti in stripped, wingless road-racing trim. Never have sports cars looked so rangy and elegant, for this was

Twenties Marquetry

PERSPECTIVE VIEW OF INTERIOR

HISPANO SUIZA SALOON

Elaborate marquetry, popular in Edwardian days, lingered on into the 1920s. These drawings made by Vanden Plas (England) for potential customers in 1920 remind one of the Lanchester at the 1919 Motor Show in London, which, H.M. George V remarked, was 'more suitable for a prostitute than a King'. The design was intended for a Hispano Suiza chassis.

This etching by Jean Emile Laboureur, circa *1926 is entitled* Jeunesse folle à Montparnasse; *in England the crew of this sports car so like a Type 43 Bugatti would have been called Bright Young Things.*

almost the last year of the narrow beaded-edge tyres, so much prettier than the fat ones which were to come. It must have been now that the artist André Derain said 'My Bugatti is more beautiful than any work of art!'

English colour schemes were more conservative than the French. Open cars might be aluminium or bright red, orange or canary yellow besides the quieter shades of beige and grey, but Barker set a private fashion lasting several years by 'graining' his coupés all over (bonnet included) to look like walnut, matt finished. It sounds terrible but a surviving example proves that in fact it looked very well. Very County, to go with good tweeds.

In Paris, where too much had proved more than enough in 1924 no Salon was held the following year. They had the big Expo instead, where all interior designers were represented and a few cars were to be seen, including a rather unconvincing 'cubist' body painted by Maurice Dufresne, and a classic coupé de ville by Labourdette. 'Metallic' paints were not new; an English car had been shown the previous year with paint which was said to glisten like granite; by spraying a thin coat of powdered aluminium upon a brown ground and covering the metal with a coat of brown varnish to match the ground Labourdette achieved a richer effect.

During the next couple of years designers learned to live with the fabric body. Sides rose to absurd heights and, some said, sank to absurd depths, by-passing the running-board. Without the latter's support front mudguards shrank to mere 'cycle-type wings' which sometimes turned with the steering, but seldom kept a car clean. Before the next Salon another revolution took place.

The 1925 cars at Olympia made previous models look old-fashioned. Learning from Hispano, Voisin and Delage, they had higher more imposing bonnets, wider doors and seats, flatter straight-line roofs, lighter pillars and increased rake to the steering column, allowing lower seats. Proportions had changed. Cars were wider because front-wheel brakes had meant increasing the front track. Fat new 'balloon' tyres now lowered the visual centre of gravity.

At the Salon, held again in 1926, the story was the same but more so. Cars sat lower on the road; pressure from sporting clients had forced designers to lower their chassis and sink foot-wells in the floor. Sides were still high (for privacy, it was said, but really to save weight on glass), but windscreens were sloped, which shortened the roof and saved weight. Weymann bodies were everywhere and two-door coupés had caught on – a fact which was perhaps more relevant than it seems: this was the year when for the first time in recorded history women's skirts rose above the knee. These were very much the cars of the Jazz Age: of the Eton Crop, backless dresses, cocktails and the Bright Young Things.

Stealthily, almost, the 'three box' body had by this time arrived. Luggage-trunks which filled the place left vacant as passengers moved forward in the wheelbase, were now framed as part of the car, accessible from inside only for the sake of strength but with outside ironmongery for looks like the dummy hood-irons on the *faux cabriolet* (sham drophead) bodies that were then so popular. Some trunks, real or sham, were covered in pony skin or even leopard to match their owners' fur coats. Meanwhile as another illustration of the way cars and high fashion interlocked at this time, there came a craze for reptilian trim. During three seasons, 1926, 1927 and 1928 when women wore snake or lizard skin shoes and handbags they bought motor cars furnished to match. Snake-catchers in India, Java and South America were hard at work, and brokers in Switzerland grew rich. Sewing-machines hummed as skins were stitched together, backed with adhesive fabric and made up into upholstery rolls, for snake-skin replaced not only veneered wood but the soft furnishings too. Cushions and squabs were made up from Calcutta and Javan lizard-skins; Karung snake, which was coarser, was used for door-cappings and finishers, and python, toughest of all, for friezes and even facias. At this end of the trade money was no object. One particular car from a Paris coachbuilder consumed fifty lizard-skins which cost 95,000 francs. Then

someone invented fake snake and the fashion dropped stone dead.

Snakes or no snakes the fashionable frenzy continued, in what with hindsight we tend to view as a Neronic fiddle concerto, a dancing mania which led to the collapse of the Great Bull Market and the Wall Street crash of 1929. Uncertain about external shapes, designers could not decide whether windscreens should be upright or sloped, V-shaped, two-piece opening or four, whether to use wheel-hugging helmet wings like a bicycle or make do

Tapestry and silver-gilt

All external brightwork on this stately Coupé de Ville Phantom I by Clark of Wolverhampton is silver plated, all internal hardware silver gilt. Built in 1927 to the order of a Hampstead businessman, the car is English provincial coachbuilding at its best. The tapestry was woven specially at Aubusson, the 'Fragonard' ceiling painted by a French artist. The sham cane and white-sidewall tyres are departures from the original black.

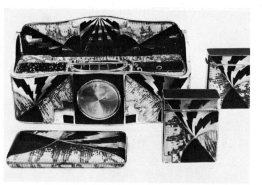

Immediately following the Exposition des Arts Décoratifs of 1925 came a vogue for snake-skin shoes, hand bags, luggage and car furnishings. One of a pair (the masculine one), this 'companion' perfectly mirrors French taste at this period. The materials include lizard-skin, lacquer, silver and silver-gilt.

with the usually hideous mudguards supplied by the manufacturers. Should there be a step or a running-board; should the body sit up on a valance or come all the way down to hub level; should the trunk be separated or integrated forming a swept and tapering tail; should wire wheels be left in the open or shrouded by decorative discs? One could still buy sports cars in polished aluminium, unpainted, and especially in France boat bodies continued; in fact Labourdette's rich clients often asked him for triple-skinned wooden construction even on coupés de ville; and very smart it looked in varnished mahogany or walnut planking fastened by fancy brass rivets. There was a craze too for angular bodies and bodies based on ancient horse-drawn vehicles – diligences, and broughams. Cellulose spray painting had taken over almost entirely from paint and varnish, though not everyone was content with anything so common. Monsieur Marcel Boussac, the silk magnate and racehorse-owner, had his 1929 Hispano-Suiza covered entirely with japanned leather with the radiator not chromed but painted to match. The result was not only very handsome but a car which was very, very quiet inside.

Interiors were sumptuous. Disappointed of their reptile skins, interior-decorators turned briefly to the new cellulose man-made fibres which were just coming on the market, such as Rayon in brightly coloured stripes and patterns. Some interiors resembled a night-club, others a fashionable apartment. Traditionalists reacted against this predictably. The King of Cambodia had his limousine de ville upholstered in yellow silk brocade, with garnish-rails and finishers in silvery leather heavily tooled with designs in bronze. A Hampstead business man, Mr. C. W. Gasque, who surrounded himself at home with French furniture, saw no reason why his taste should degringolate when he rode out, and commissioned a French interior for his 1927 Rolls-Royce Phantom I brougham

from Clark of Wolverhampton. Drawing eclectically on Louis XV, Louis XVI and Empire elements he furnished the interior with a couch in the Egyptian taste and commissioned special Aubusson tapestries for the upholstery. He also brought over a French artist to paint cherubs and roses on the ceiling and on the satinwood panelling of the doors and division, the latter with bow-fronted cabinet for drinks.

Only a couple more years and the luxurious smart world of the motoring 1920s would be engulfed by the Wall Street smash. Meanwhile there was still time for gilt and rosewood, ivory, rock-crystal, parchment (like that used by Bugatti's father Carlo in his famous furniture), lacquer and shagreen. In 1928 Sonia Terk Delaunay, wife of the Orphic Robert, posed mannequins wearing her 'simultaneous' colour-schemes against a yellow and black Talbot-Darracq drop head coupé, a similar car to the one offered as prize for a duelling-pistol championship at Gastinne Rennette's gallery beside the Petit Palais. Only one thing it lacked, and that could be readily supplied: a glass mascot designed by René Lalique, the ultimate touch to a smart car in the Art Deco decade. The idea of illuminated mascots is said to have been inspired by what must be the largest piece of motoring art or publicity ever made. It seems unbelievable today but André Citroën actually obtained permission to use the Eiffel Tower as an enormous flashing advertisement hoarding. Thousands of electric bulbs flashed on and off, making comets swoop down the Tower, giving place to the Citroën chevron trademark.

Whether inspired in this instance by André Citroën's vulgarity or not, Lalique (1860–1945) had long been famous for moulded and engraved glass, from a Symbolist beginning before the turn of the century and on through the inspired decadence of Art Nouveau. He had also a name for *bijouterie*, semi-precious adornments of gold, silver, bronze, glass and shells that Alphonse Mucha might well have designed for Sarah Bernhardt or for one of those goddesses in an early automobile poster. He was of course no stranger to cars, and it will be remembered that it was he who designed the first two at least of the bronze-and-enamel plaques for the Targa Florio. Gradually glass became Lalique's speciality, even, almost the trademark of Art Deco as the Paris style of the 1920s came to be called. And for later bronze plaques in his Targa Florio series (e.g., 1924, 1929) Vincenzo Florio went not to Lalique but to Henry Dropsy (b. 1885).

Best known for his moulded glass car mascots (left and below), René Lalique (1860–1945) first made his name in Paris as a goldsmith and jeweller. It was to him therefore that Vincenzo Florio went for the original targa *or plaque for his Targa Florio races (above). Cast in gold, chased and decorated with coloured enamels, they measured 11 by 8 inches and cost 5,000 gold francs. The mascots made from plain or opalescent glass, with or without a light in the plinth, became popular by 1928.*

HISPANO-SUIZA

The Stylists

Art and architecture in motorcar design

NOT FOR NOTHING are the years 1920–1930 known as the Vintage Period. During that time as we have seen the smart world was concerned with smart cars; and their appointments were chosen, in France and occasionally Britain, to accord with fashionable taste and the artistic ideas of the time.

The Depression that followed the Wall Street crash of 1929 wiped out hundreds of car manufacturers, and coachbuilders by the dozen. It also seriously quelled the people whose taste and extravagance had created the *voitures de luxe* on which new ideas were tried out. Tremendous courage was displayed by Marc Birkigt, head of Hispano-Suiza, always smartest of French makes, who doubled the number of cylinders and brought out a model regardless of cost, the great 9½-litre V-Twelve, which was soon increased to 11½ litres. Rolls-Royce continued to prosper, selling not only the 'small' 20–25 hp but also the Phantom II which in short Continental form, its radiator on the plane of the axle, was the most handsome Rolls-Royce ever minted. Ettore Bugatti persevered with his Royale, a superb eight-cylinder 12¾-litre creation as large as a small lorry, of which only six or seven were built and only two were sold to the public. One of these, a coupé de ville designed by young Jean Bugatti, was of superbly elegant proportions with tiny cab body and wings as long

as a contemporary mannequin's legs. Features of the Royale were carried over into the 5-litre, one of the smartest French cars of all time; but the beauty of both cars lay in their lines and their engineering. Bugatti, an artist like his father and brother, left interior design to the factory, and it was seldom very distinguished; he did however allow himself elaborate external luggage-trunks, sometimes covered in pony skin – or even leopard.

Duesenberg in America created a huge and expensive chassis which generated some excellent coachwork, particularly of the 'twin cowl phaeton' type; but the East

Hispano-Suiza weathered the Depression by making ever more luxurious cars. The post-Art Deco publicity drawing by René Ravo (opposite) makes daring use of perspective, the car and the tilted horizon line having the same vanishing point. Below: *the acme of luxurious motoring, a 1934 twelve-cylinder 11 litre* 68 Bis.

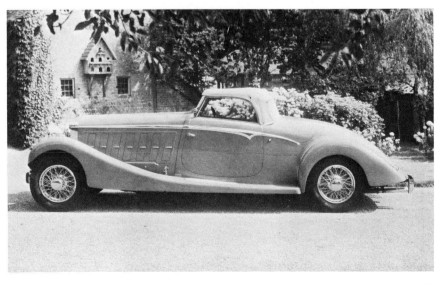

Above: *Bred for the Mille Miglia 1,000-miles race on the open road, Alfa Romeo two-seaters of this period achieved a grace which has never been excelled. Also graceful, and less extreme than many French coachbuilt bodies of the late 1930s are the Lago Talbots below, although the artist has exaggerated their length.*

Coast families for whom it was planned held back, scenting vulgarity, and most of the cars were furnished with Hollywood in mind. In France and America both, *chic* was giving way to flamboyance. Smart designs were still to be had, notably from the long, low, rakish D 8 Delage chassis with its vast bonnet and shallow 'letter-box' windscreen. These performed well and were enjoyed by those sitting tall enough to see out; but their 'image' was distinctly show-biz. Is there not an analogy with the chocolate-box slickness of contemporary painters like Jean-Gabriel Domergue, whose luscious lovelies were to be seen on every magazine cover?

Sports car designers continued to make rakish, balanced designs; there were the Bugatti Type 55, and the Alfa Romeos from Milan. Sleek road cars were still to be had when Europe surfaced after the Depression; there were new models from Hispano and Voisin and Delage, lower, faster, slinkier and every bit as luxurious as those which had gone before; the Delage D 8 100 had the longest bonnet and the lowest

lines of all. But the old magic had gone. Now it was not *chic* that counted, but performance and a certain commercialized glamour. Cars were relegated from the covers of *Vogue* to their place in the motoring papers. They were no longer in the mainstream of taste as they had been briefly in the 1920s, in fact they developed a provincialism of their own. Oddly and rather sadly, small traces of Art Nouveau lingered on: an Egyptian touch here, a Ziggurat there, a sunburst stitched into the lining of a door. In mass-produced cars the Bloats set in. As external lines grew weaker and more banal, odious chromium 'flashes' were stuck on in the hope of relieving the tedium. Engines moved forward, doors came down to the running boards and the latter sometimes vanished altogether. All was set for the slab-sided post-war look.

A dreadful lack of adventure beset interior designers. Artists and decorators kept aloof and manufacturers, from fear of offending the mass market succumbed to drab uniformity. They might have drawn inspiration from one of their own kind, but from a previous age: Algernon E. Berriman, sometime managing director of Daimlers, and author of the best-selling book *Motoring* (Methuen, London 1914): 'Since the enclosed car has become so universally popular, the internal decoration has assumed a much increased importance, and anyone who is selecting materials for the upholstery should bear in mind that the colouring thereof will form an ever-present foreground to the distance provided by nature. The fundamental tones of the countryside are green and brown, and as the natural shades that are thus provided are so much superior to anything that can be artificially produced, it is on the whole preferable to select a contrast to them as the basis of a colour scheme for a closed car.

'The interior itself, however, should not be subject to contrast, although changes of shade are desirable. Especially should the ceiling be lighter than the floor, which latter also may, with advantage, be made darker than the walls. Red is pre-eminently a cheerful colour, and it has warmth. Pinks, ranging from salmon to rose, form an artistic contrast to the surroundings, but the blue pinks must always be avoided. Blue in itself is soothing when well chosen, but otherwise is apt to be cold. A pale turquoise is as artistic as any, but is not easily obtainable in the right shade.

The Edwardian and Art Deco years have been treated in some detail because they represent the two periods during which the design and interior decoration of cars attracted the attention of specialists outside the manufacturing and coachbuilding industries, and the customer's taste was reflected in the finished article. Thoroughgoing 'bespoke' bodywork, of the sort Berriman speaks of, lasted long enough for the ivory and royal blue, 'amber against turquoise and jade in a setting of old rose', to be replaced by Jazz Age elements – lizardskin, lacquer from Dunand, and Lalique glass, but such fashionable frivolities hardly survived the Great Depression. They had their last fling at the 1928 Paris Salon. Increasingly from then on cars were to reflect the taste – or banality – of manufacturers and coachbuilders rather than that of the individual customer. Individuality indeed was seen as a disadvantage, entailing higher depreciation, and expensive cars then as now lost their value quickly enough in standard form. Only now, when antique and classic cars are collected, have elaborate interiors come into their own, increasing rather than detracting from the value of the cars they adorn.

Avant-garde exteriors have tended to be more acceptable, especially when designed to improve performance, e.g., by streamlining. Aerodynamicists have been called in from time to time to reduce wind-resistance, especially on competition cars. From designing airships for the Zeppelin company during the First World War, Paul

Below, top picture: A Duesenberg twin-cowl phaeton on the supercharged SJ chassis represented many a film star's ambition. This 1932 example has coachwork by Walker. The Chrysler Corporation made many experiments before launching their Airflow models, of which a 1935 one is shown below. Most of the benefit from 'streamlining' was swallowed by that tall open radiator grille.

Above: *An interesting study in ellipses, this Talbot Lago coupé by Figoni et Falaschi is more restrained than many of their productions.* Right: *By 1951 mudguards had become part of the car and the 'habitacle' much wider, as witness this 356 Porsche.* Far right: *The DS 19 Citroën, appearing in 1955, has required little alteration; it went impossibly fast on very little power thanks to smooth contours and good separation.*

Jaray turned his attention to cars during the peace. He worked with Rumpler on some rather *outré* streamlined saloons, and after moving to Switzerland became consultant to Chrysler during their Airflow experiments. The result was a model which, although clumsy and garish in production form, did show some improvements in speed and fuel consumption. His *Rennlimousine* for Adler, however, raced at Le Mans in 1937, went indecently fast (80 mph on 40 bhp) and should have shamed the world's motor manufacturers into imitation, though it did not. Jean Andreau, in France, was another successful practitioner. He designed George Eyston's Land Speed Record car, Thunderbolt, which did 357 mph. His ideas appeared also on some sporting Peugeots, and, greatly vulgarised, on Delage and Delahaye chassis with coachwork by people

like Figoni et Falaschi, unkindly pronounced in some circles as Phoney and Flashy. The motor industry as a whole has always regarded aerodynamics as a lot of fuss about nothing, shutting its eyes and ears to the advantages of good penetration, flush windows and a smooth undertray. The honourable exceptions, such as Citroën, Lotus and Porsche, are reaping just rewards for offering cars which go unusually fast on a small expenditure of fuel.

Accepting the adage that onlookers see most of the game, it seems odd that architects, whose job after all is to reconcile man and his environment, have not been more often consulted. They might have avoided some of the more glaring follies, such as blind spots, scuttles too high for most women and all children to peer over, and back seats too cramped for anyone but a legless dwarf or bicrural amputee. Very few examples come to mind of cars designed by a chartered architect, but they do exist. In the early 1920s Sir John Siddeley, of Armstrong-Siddeley Motors, made a promising young English architect, Ronald A. Duncan, ARIBA, responsible for the looks of a proposed £100 light car with an air-cooled V-twin engine. The result was a notably clean design which made the most of the short wheelbase by taking the body-sides down flush, without the valances then fashionable. The seating was also unusual, with the driver placed centrally in front and two passenger seats behind. In this way everyone had the best possible view and it was impossible to over-load the 1-litre engine. Unfortunately the three-seater Stoneleigh died almost before reaching the market, killed by competition from William Morris's cut-price Morris Cowley and Herbert Austin's famous Seven. Duncan's essay in car design was not forgotten, however, and some years later he was retained as architect for an interesting four-seater convertible saloon Austin Seven with counterbalanced folding roof called the Merlyn. Again the doors ran full depth, without running-boards, while the colour scheme might have appealed to A. E. Berriman: black bonnet, wings and top, the body panelled in pale grey 'python-skin' fabric and with cherry-red leather seats.

Some years after Duncan's Merlyn Austin Seven of 1928 a very distinguished architect, none other than Professor Walter Gropius (1883–1969), one of the founders of the Bauhaus at Weimar, was commissioned by the German firm of Adler to design them a drophead coupé or cabriolet. Professor Gropius left Germany for Harvard University when the Nazis came to power, so the car must date from before 1933; but this type of smart but solid drophead bodywork remained popular on the Continent until well after the Second World War.

If the list of architect-designers is short, that of one-man design teams, known first as consultants but latterly as stylists, is long. They have flourished especially in the United States, where an early styling studio, LeBaron, was established by Tom Hibbard, Howard ('Dutch') Darrin and Ray Dietrich in 1921. Hibbard and Darrin set off for Paris the following year, where they opened an agency for the Minerva car but quickly found themselves designing bodies for private clients, for the industry and for other coachbuilders. When Hibbard returned to the United States Dutch Darrin continued as consultant and coach-

Below: *The Packard V12 was one of the best cars of its day. This 1938 coupé de ville is by LeBaron; traditional bodywork looks slightly uneasy with a forward-mounted radiator.*

builder, making exceedingly elegant bodies in partnership with a banker named Fernandez, their firm being Fernandez & Darrin. Big corporations seem often to be unsure of their own judgement, so that freelances like Hibbard and Darrin were briefed at one time or another by many concerns, including Ford, General Motors, as well as smaller companies like Moon Diana, Franklin and Stutz. Hibbard eventually became head of styling at Ford.

Harley Earl, afterwards famous as head of the General Motors 'Art and Color Section' which was created for him, began life as a member of his family's coachbuilding firm in Los Angeles. He was brought to the attention of Alfred P. Sloan, president of General Motors, by Lawrence Fisher, general manager of Cadillac when the Corporation was planning the LaSalle car in 1925. Named, like the Cadillac, after an *ancien régime* French explorer and soldier of fortune, the LaSalle was to be a semi-sporting make bridging the gap between that luxurious model and the rather staid Buick. Harley Earl was put in charge of the project, and quickly produced an extremely good-looking range. 'The Hispano was the car I was in love with from stem to stern,' he is on record as saying, and he took Birkigt's tall, opulent and perfectly proportioned radiator as his starting point. This gave a high bonnet line, which Earl continued with little change into a high 'elbow', a radical departure for American roadsters and tourers at that time, which were low in the flank. Empty, they looked fine, but the occupants sat very high and had sometimes the air of sea-lions popping up through the ice. Earl imported a European presentation, but combined it with the lean, clean flanks and flush valances that were such an excellent feature of US

design in the mid-1920s. He literally made the best of both worlds.

Harley Earl presided over an expanding empire of GM stylists until 1962 when he handed over to William Mitchell, whom we shall return to later.

A history of American styling must await another occasion, but a little name-dropping is irresistible. One thinks of the Russian emigré, Alexis de Sakhnoffsky, whose smart presentation drawings introduced the idea of automobile styling to readers of *Esquire* in the great opening years of that magazine. A good publicist, he was also a talented body designer. He freelanced for Continental coachbuilders like Vanden Plas before leaving for the United States in 1927, where he joined the Hayes Body Company. He had a great success with his L29 Cord coupé for that concern, built in the hope that Cord would adopt it as standard. The low-slung straight-eight Cord lent itself superbly to his treatment, with its low roof, swept elbow line, absence of running-boards and finned roadster boot. De Sakhnoffsky drove the car from Milwaukee to New York and from Le Havre to Paris, where he won first prize at a concours d'élégance, then repeated this success at Beaulieu s/Mer and Monte Carlo.

Gorden Buehrig was the designer identified in most people's minds with Cord, but his was the later Cord with V8 engine, models 810 and 812, one of the all-time originals. Adopting the Edwardian practice of hingeing the bonnet at the back, with 'wrap-around' radiator intake without ornate grille, low build and 'pontoon' front wings it was well ahead of its time, and extremely influential. Unfortunately the 810/812 Cords were bedevilled by a complex and unreliable gear-shift

Harley Earle's first assignment on joining General Motors in 1925 was to design the new LaSalle, a model midway between the existing Cadillac and Buick ranges. His favourite car, he proclaimed, was the Hispano-Suiza; so the LaSalle (below right) was designed round the noble Hispano radiator. The same form was retained by Hispano on almost all models, including the 'Ballot Hispano' (below) planned in 1931 when they took over the Ballot concern. This striking catalogue project is by P. Martin.

Left: *Gordon Buehrig designed the front-wheel-drive 810 Cord roadster, with retractable headlamps, in 1935. Below: Gurney, Nutting & Co., of London were responsible for some very attractive close-coupled and drophead bodywork during the 1930s, of which this Phantom III is a late example. Their designer, J. J. McNeill, afterwards went to James Young & Co. of Bromley. Note in this picture the rear-hinged door, separate trunk and the slightly valanced front wings, typical of 1936. They later became deeper and clumsier.*

mechanism and the model life was short. Buehrig, born in 1903, had been with Harley Earl at General Motors before moving to Stutz and then to Duesenberg as designer to that company and E. L. Cord's empire. Later he passed to Ford's styling department in Detroit. When he retired, around 1965, gigantism had so far overtaken that company that the engineering and styling departments employed, he said, some 12,000 people 'plus a battery of computers'. The day of the one-man design team had apparently passed – except in Italy and to a small extent England, where individual talent still counted.

Design during the 1930s took a different direction from that which it had during the Vintage period, because new clients wanted different things. Proportions changed because engines moved forward and bodies grew larger. Flamboyance broke out, especially in France. American companies made some clean designs: there has seldom been a better-looking drophead than the 1933 US Ford, with a shield-shaped radiator, which replaced the drophead based on the Model A. The Lincoln Zephyr was clean – and widely copied, even after the war, as witness the Jowett Javelin. Clean designs in the US continued even up to the Second World War. The 1939 Packard Clipper, stripped of its chrome and then painted khaki, could almost have passed for a post-war Italian. The interplay of design to and fro across the Atlantic could be the theme for another book. Europe meanwhile had a moratorium on ideas. The restrained 'London School', razor-edged and elegant, which reached its zenith with the Barker

tourers of 1925–7 and the Continental Phantom IIs, no longer had the old chassis proportions to work with; and the James Young designer, A. F. McNeill, who in his early days with Gurney Nutting and subsequently with James Young themselves, had been so successful with Sedanca coupés, now, like his colleagues, had to rethink the architecture of luxury cars.

The first few London Motor Shows after World War II produced some odd aesthetic gymnastics. Old-established coach builders, anxious to build wide but horrified by slab sides, compromised, giving rise to a 'melted sealing-wax' look.

Inside, the bodies on the coachwork stands were impeccable – beautifully sewn, exquisitely finished, tricked out with divisions and cabinets veneered by experienced, dedicated craftsmen. And usually monumentally dull, in the worst of

Publicity for the London Motor Show was seldom very distinguished, but this poster by A. E. Marty from 1933 is an exception. (Above). Later exhibitions migrated from Olympia to the big new building at Earls Court, where this photo of Sir Bernard Docker's gold-starred Daimler was taken. (Below). The proportions of this vast straight eight were skilfully handled by O. F. Rivers, chief designer of Hooper & Company, who devised the spear-shaped panel between flowing wing-line and waist.

good taste. A single happy exception springs to mind from those early shows: a Mark VI Bentley by Rippon, of Huddersfield, painted what might be called 'rich Air Force' blue, the cabinetwork silver grey in bleached sycamore; a handsome change from the ubiquitous walnut.

While austerity ruled the life of the ordinary motorist, the luxury products of the coachbuilders continued to find customers. James Young and Company, based in Bromley, continued doing special interior work for Indian and other Eastern poten-

tates until well after World War II, sometimes with solid gold fittings, about which they were understandably coy; and Messrs. Hooper & Company built a series of remarkable Daimlers for Sir Bernard Docker, the chairman of their parent company, during the early 1950s. These bodies were built regardless of expense as though to prove that there was nothing that a Maharajah of 1910 might have ordered which could not be produced by British craftsmen in the immediate post-war period. The climactic motor car was a Daimler straight-eight with special limousine body designed by the Hooper chief designer, Mr. Osmond F. Rivers, and built in accordance with the taste of Lady Docker. The theme was gold. The inside was furnished in the richest possible golden yellow silk brocade specially woven at Lyons and all interior brightwork was gilt. The outside of the body was black, with little gold stars forming an over all pattern, each star painted on individually by the heraldic artist employed by Hoopers at that time for crests or armorial bearings on door panels. In the boot of this immense car was a set of fitted suitcases made from alligator-hide, with gilt locks and fittings. Even the plated corrugations of the Daimler false radiator shell were gilt, as were the lamps. A problem arose concerning the bumpers, a very necessary feature as the car was to be used continually in town and for touring. Chromium would have clashed hideously, and bright gold would have been too much. A compromise arrived at matt gold. The car was a magnificent folly, politically and economically injudicious in those days of Stafford Crippsian austerity perhaps, but as a showpiece for the designer, panel-beaters, painters, joiners, cabinet-makers, trimmers and purveyors of such luxury goods as crystal, ebony hairbrushes, gold pencils and the like it was absolutely unrivalled, and quite exquisitely made. Perhaps the last word on this, the ultimate in conventional coachwork de luxe, was a remark overheard during Press day on the Hooper stand. 'I suppose,' said a cynic referring to the suitcases, 'you dye your alligator black and then shoot it.'

Even during the 1960s there were still coachbuilders' stands at Earls Court and the Salon, but one saw hardly a trace of adventure. No exciting new fabrics and finishes even on Show cars and single commissions: everywhere the same impeccable, durable, unendurable 'best quality furniture hide' and 'finest West of England cloth'; and everywhere that glossy walnut which used to look like plastic and which is now plastic printed to look like walnut. Perhaps if the coachbuilders had shown some individuality and called in some artists, they would be alive and prosperous today.

Fortunately for us all ossification was not universal. A revolution was on the way, and this revolution originated in Italy. As the post-war recovery set in and manufacture shrank to a mere three constructors, only one of whom built in bulk, customers cast around for novelty. Italy at that time was rich in artistic talent and well supplied with artisans. One or two coachbuilders before the war had seen this need and supplied it. One of these was Pinin Farina, who designed and sold smart new bonnet and radiator grille units for Fiat 500 and 1100 models, replacing the mass-produced article. Why not, the trade wondered, do the same thing again but extend the idea to the car as a whole? Why not make limited-production specials using cheaply available parts? These *fuori serie* Fiats caught on. To drive an 1100 *speciale* was as good as wearing clothes from a Paris couturier.

By this time, of course, Fiat like other big car firms were employing 'unitary construction', the largest change the 1930s had brought. No longer (except in short

production runs) did cars consist of a body and chassis; the body was a steel load-bearing structure like a ship's hull or aeroplane fuselage. So to make a special meant throwing away the unitary structure evolved with great planning by Fiat, and designing a new hull, low, sleek and seductive, for an engine, transmission and running-gear bought new from the factory. Designers, panel-beaters, welders and trimmers abounded in Turin. Soon the only question was which of the many specials to buy: Farina, Bertone, Vignale, Viotti, Sivocci, Ghia . . . The choice was wide. Models were created with astounding speed; they were without doubt the smartest thing on wheels. Exhibited at motor shows in Geneva, Frankfurt, Paris, London and Turin they made standard models dowdy overnight. They had great purity of line, contrasting amazingly with contemporary paintings of the New York school, the organic extravagance of Arshile Gorky, for instance, or the broken surfaces of De Kooning, the exuberant accidentals contrived by Jackson Pollock. They were cool, cool – more like the 'white writing' of Mark Tobey.

The significance of this Italian revolution twenty-five years ago is that for almost the first time in history the problems of motor car design were approached from an

Many British manufacturers since the war have gone to Italian designers for their bodywork, rather strangely ignoring the undoubted talent to be found in native concerns. The 1970 A.C. 428 (top) was by Frua, and the 1969 Jensen Interceptor, virtually a hatchback body, by Vignale (lower picture) both of Turin.

The Pininfarina Touch

Young Pininfarina left his brother's firm, Stabilimenti Farina, and set up as Carrozzeria Pinin Farina, also at Turin. Assisted by his son Sergio and son-in-law Renzo Carli, the business grew in international standing after the war, not only designing special bodywork for rich customers but also supplying designs to manufacturers all over the world. Skilful presentation is an essential part of publicity and salesmanship; and so, to supplement the posters and catalogue illustrations reproduced elsewhere in this book we publish some drawings from the Pininfarina studios.

Right, top to bottom:
1949: an early essay in full-width bodywork for H. H. Aly Khan. Variations of this extremely graceful 1956 coupé were made for several manufacturers. This car is the Lancia Appia.
Ferrari 410 Superamerica 1963, with notably small horizontal air intake grille.
By 1968 aerofoils and roll-over bars were equally in the news. Here on an Alfa Romeo P/33 gran sport the two features are skilfully combined.
Below: This design for a Peugeot 104 was made in 1978. An interesting reversion to narrow two-seaters. . . .

SPECIAL BODY ON *Alfa Romeo* EXPRESSELY DESIGNED FOR S.A. Prince **ALI KHAN**

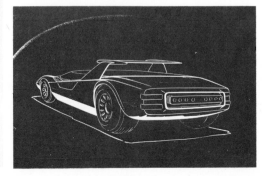

aesthetic standpoint. Hitherto manufacturers had provided a plot and invited body specialists to build on it. Now the artists moved in, discarding the features they did not like, such as high floors, high sills and small windows. But these were no airy-fairy idealists from an ivory tower. They were practical hard-driving citizens of Turin and Milan, brought up in an atmosphere of fast cars and racing. Alpine passes led off in every direction. They could not move from Turin to Milan without taking the *autostrada*. Even the police had motor sport in their veins; fast cars were intended to be driven fast, and when they saw an exciting car coming, even in the rush hour, they held up other traffic and smilingly waved it on. Special bodywork therefore created special cars, low, handy and practical, and there was a unity of design which extended to the decor, seats and furnishings, with which these engineers seemed equally at home. They lived in a different world from certain British designers who had never delighted in motoring and in some cases could not drive a car.

Clearly, this unified approach to automobile design was what the manufacturers wanted, for everywhere they sat at the Italians' feet. They gave them contracts, bought their brains. In return Pinin Farina (now Pininfarina, one word), Bertone, Vignale, Michelotti and others evolved ingenious pastiches, brilliant parodies of any national style to suit all tastes. Their customers included Peugeot, Lancia, Ferrari and indeed the British Motor Corporation. Italian influence spread to the United States, where Harley Earl's successor at General Motors, William Mitchell, made some very clean designs. His Buick Riviera, with its crisp silhouette and unclut-

tered façade, showed strong Pininfarina influence. Several of Mitchell's classic designs, including the Toronado, Sting Ray and Mako Shark, showed traces of the semi-razor-edged panelling identified with the London coachbuilders. That the Italians did not have a monopoly of pastiche is evident from the work of the French-American, Raymond Loewy, who is credited with the Sunbeam Talbot Ten for the Rootes Group, a very Savile Row exercise, as well as one hundred per cent American automobiles for Studebaker, the last of which, the Avanti, introduced the popular 'coke bottle' line and was, incidentally, the car which Ian Fleming preferred to all others, despite his hero James Bond's involvements with Bentley and Aston Martin. Yet it is Italian influence which has remained predominant throughout the world. Today international styling is very largely taken care of by Giorgetto Giugiaro (born 1937) whose historic designs include the BMW 3200 CS, Alfa Romeo Giulia Sprint GT, Alfa Giulia Kanguro, Mazda 1000, Fiat 850 Spider and Lamborghini Miura. Now operating his own studio, ItalDesign, he has supplied influential drawings to Renault and has been responsible for the Alfa Sud, the current VW range, and the Lotus Esprit.

Below: No motor car could look more British than this R-Type Continental Bentley by H. J. Mulliner, even though the virtually pillarless window treatment originated in Paris during the early 1930s. Other influences are the 'high wing line' of contemporary Young saloons. This car's 'fastback' roof recalls a streamlined Speed Six Bentley made by Gurney Nutting for Woolf Barnato about 1930, probably an early work of the same designer, A. F. McNeill. Bottom picture: In the 1972 Chevrolet Corvette Sting Ray William Mitchell's department aimed at brutality and machismo. They succeeded.

Art for Enthusiasts 1

Gordon Crosby, Bryan de Grineau and Geo Ham

Geo Ham (1900–1972) could always be depended on for a striking poster. This watercolour is a sketch for the French Grand Prix poster in 1938. It reflects not only contemporary single-seater designs but also the Derby-Miller of Mrs. Gwenda Stewart which held the lap record at Montlhéry.

DURING THE 1920s and 1930s while motor cars were finding their shape, coach-builders exercising their art and the majority of painters and sculptors preoccupied with non-figurative work, the motoring papers enjoyed great popularity with a public interested in technicalities and sport. This was nourished on both sides of the Channel by artists who in the main had watched things develop since the days of the chain-drive monsters. In Britain motor racing, prohibited on the public roads except in Ulster and the Isle of Man, meant Brooklands Track and various hill-climb meetings held either more or less clandestinely on the road, or at Shelsley Walsh, a privately owned hill in Worcestershire at which the Midland Automobile Club organized several meetings a year. Only during the early 1930s was Donington Park, near Derby, brought into play by Fred Craner of the Derby & District Motor Club, so that eventually British enthusiasts had the chance to see Grand Prix racing to the highest international standards on English soil. Nonetheless the British motoring papers managed to keep their readers in touch with events elsewhere, and the influence of the men engaged by *The Motor* and *The Autocar* in the early days is still very much to be seen.

The story of British car illustration begins about 1903, a time when in France René Vincent was already making his name. By some unlikely circumstance the management of Temple Press Ltd., proprietors of *The Motor*, had engaged a young man named Guy Lipscombe to take charge of the art department. Perhaps they had seen and admired some of Lipscombe's hunting-cum-motor car scenes in the sporting papers; however that may be they signed him up and appeared proud in a rather philistine way of having a real artist on the strength who looked and dressed like a character from *La Bohème*. The only available portrait of Guy Lipscombe shows a shy, good-looking young man in velvet jacket posing, palette in hand, beside an attractive Sargent-like portrait of a girl. Very soon, though, the management found another use for his talents. Technical illustrations in the early motoring papers had consisted either of photographs or of engineers' blueprints redrawn, neither of which conveyed very much to the ordinary reader who wished to know what he was looking at when obliged, in the words of the popular song 'Get out and get under, get out and get under, get under the automobile.' Lispcombe was therefore detailed to floor himself and make perspective drawings of such vital items as clutch withdrawal mechanism, gear-selectors and so on. These were the first in a long line of technical perspectives which were to culminate in the 'X-ray' engine drawings of L. C. Cresswell, Max Millar, Gédo in

One of the earliest English motoring artists was Guy Lipscombe (born circa 1883), who was engaged by The Motor *to take charge of their art department in about 1903. His oil paintings include a study of Tate's 1908 Grand Prix Mercedes on the Brooklands banking (below). Bottom:* Another artist on The Motor *was Ernest L. Ford, who drew this vivid impression from the cockpit of a Vauxhall at the 1914 Tourist Trophy in the Isle of Man. The caption (from* The Car*) reads 'Climbing Snaefell: a driver's outlook. (All he sees is a little strip of road 100 yards ahead.)'*

France, Theo Page, Brian Hatton and other current practitioners of the magic art.

Guy Lipscombe's first love was oil painting. He must have been the first to paint cars on the Brooklands banking, and fortunately at least one of these has survived, a study of Tate's 1908 Grand Prix Mercedes in the collection of Mr. Anthony S. Heal. He also made some dramatic posters for insurance companies, showing racing cars on a collision course with the viewer at a range of a couple of yards: the wide-angle lens approach that the Frenchman Georges Hamel (Geo Ham) was to

exploit for Montlhéry track posters during the 1920s. There are also some non-racing Lipscombe studies of cars, but a large and important canvas which used to hang in the Royal Automobile Club in London seems to have disappeared.

Contemporary with Lipscombe on *The Motor,* although joining somewhat later, was a young artist named John A. Bryan, who eventually took over from him and was to become famous in later years as Bryan de Grineau, having at his wife's suggestion adopted an old family name for professional purposes. John Bryan's work included technical drawings for descriptions of new models and motor show reports, but he was also sent to Brooklands to cover races and record attempts. The early free-hand reports were perhaps a little stilted, but he made some extremely dramatic drawings, one which still lingers in the memory being an impression of L. G. Hornsted's monumental skid in the 21-litre 'Blitzen' Benz which lasted for three-quarters of a mile. The car slowly spun until it was heading straight for the lip of the Brooklands banking, and at that point as he subsequently told the writer, Hornsted realized that as the cause of the skid had been the bursting of a rear tyre, which had wrapped itself round the chain-drive sprocket, the wheels would be locked and he could therefore select any gear as though he were standing still. 'So I put in reverse, revved up, let in the clutch and shot downwards off the track into the sewage-farm.' The speed lines and gyratory wheel-tracks make a rather spirited drawing. John Bryan also rode as a passenger at Brooklands in order to give readers an idea of what it was like to be a riding mechanic, whose job included pumping up fuel pressure and keeping an eye on the pressure and temperature gauges.

Another gifted black-and-white man on *The Motor* in those pre-war days was Ernest L. Ford. He too did technical and sporting drawings before leaving the magazine's publishers, Temple Press, to open a studio of his own. It was during this freelance period that he went to the Isle of Man to cover the R.A.C. Tourist Trophy races for *The Car* in 1914 and while there experienced a high-speed lap round the mountainous circuit which is still used for the motorcycle T.T. races. He rode with one of the Vauxhall drivers, probably A. J. Hancock, in one of L. H. Pomeroy's designs, which were probably the fastest machines there. Ford produced an excellent cockpit impression from this ride, and also during the race a powerful drawing of

M.P. TEN BOSCH, "FIAT", SPINS RIGHT ROUND AT THE MEMBERS BRIDGE IN THE 1ST MOUNTAIN HANDICAP.

A.G. DOBBS, "RILEY", BROADSIDES AT THE FORK IN THE 3RD MOUNTAIN HANDICAP.

P.N WHITEHEAD, "ERA", SIDE-SWIPES THE BARRIER IN THE 2ND MOUNTAIN HANDICAP.

THE SAME COMPLAINT TROUBLES BOTH GREAT AND SMALL CARS IN THE GOLD STAR RACE — OLIVER BERTRAM "BARNATO-HASSAN" AND A.P. SAMUEL, "M.G" BOTH SHEDDING TYRE TREADS IN THE RAILWAY STRAIGHT —

BRYAN DE GRINEAU BROOKLANDS 36

Bryan de Grineau (1882–1957) incarnated the spirit of Brooklands for readers of The Motor *as F. Gordon Crosby did for those of* The Autocar. *These vivid sketches were made in 1936. De Grineau joined* The Motor *as John A. Bryan soon after 1905.*

Over page: F. Gordon Crosby (1885–1942) remains the acknowledged master of motoring art, whether reporting current events or, as here, re-creating a historical incident. This dramatic drawing (one of the 'Meteors of Road and Track' series) shows Gabriel and his mechanic changing a tyre on their De Dietrich while F. Szisz, winner of the 1906 French Grand Prix passes in his Renault. Crosby's mechanical details always remain crisp, unshrouded by 'pork'.

Hancock's Vauxhall in the act of capsizing. On the outbreak of war, Ford joined the Royal Naval Air Service as a pilot but went on drawing until a serious crash put him in hospital. It was his sketches, published by the Admiralty to illustrate points of airmanship and tactics, that pilots used to study on the walls of hangars and adjutant's office. Ernest Ford's accident prevented him from returning to motoring art, but a number of old names were on parade including John Bryan, now styled Bryan

de Grineau, who had finished the war as a major in the Royal Artillery, and went back to Temple Press on a retainer. Also back with Temple Press was an old colleague of his on the art side, L. Graham Davies, but Davies had now become Paris Correspondent for all Temple Press journals and was producing no more drawings.

Bryan de Grineau was a considerable personality, good company and an excellent travelling companion. The new name was undoubtedly an asset but, as Rodney

The Monaco Grand Prix established 'round-the-houses' racing in 1929. Here Bryan de Grineau captures a Type 51 Bugatti and Monza Alfa Romeo as they take the hairpin by the Hotel Terminus. Below, left: The Sunday night deadline on The Motor, *which came out on Tuesdays, meant that Bryan de Grineau had to work at top speed; but his work remained fresh and interesting. This sketch shows a Bugatti vs Lagonda duel in the 1935 Ulster Tourist Trophy. Below, right: In this Bryan de Grineau study of C. J. P. Dodson's M.G. Magnette in the 1934 Ulster T.T. at Newtonards one can almost feel and hear the rain.*

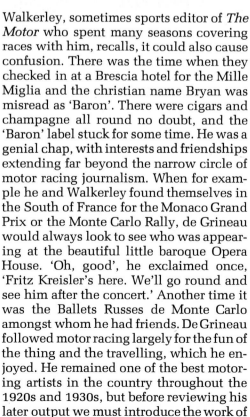

Walkerley, sometimes sports editor of *The Motor* who spent many seasons covering races with him, recalls, it could also cause confusion. There was the time when they checked in at a Brescia hotel for the Mille Miglia and the christian name Bryan was misread as 'Baron'. There were cigars and champagne all round no doubt, and the 'Baron' label stuck for some time. He was a genial chap, with interests and friendships extending far beyond the narrow circle of motor racing journalism. When for example he and Walkerley found themselves in the South of France for the Monaco Grand Prix or the Monte Carlo Rally, de Grineau would always look to see who was appearing at the beautiful little baroque Opera House. 'Oh, good', he exclaimed once, 'Fritz Kreisler's here. We'll go round and see him after the concert.' Another time it was the Ballets Russes de Monte Carlo amongst whom he had friends. De Grineau followed motor racing largely for the fun of the thing and the travelling, which he enjoyed. He remained one of the best motoring artists in the country throughout the 1920s and 1930s, but before reviewing his later output we must introduce the work of

his rival, F. Gordon Crosby, who must have joined *The Autocar* soon after de Grineau joined *The Motor*. Both magazines used the definite article in those days – until the 1960s in fact, when as a cynic untruly remarked 'they stopped printing definite articles'.

Frederick Gordon Crosby, known as Freddie to his friends, was born in 1885. He worked as a very young man in the drawing office of the Daimler Company at Coventry before joining the staff of *The Autocar* as a sort of artistic dogsbody. His early pictorial drawings were not particularly distinguished but he did soon score, we are told, by making one of the earliest ever 'exploded' drawings in order to explain the workings of a B.T.H. magneto, which his technical training fully qualified him to do. He soon found his feet artistically and began the long series of paintings in various media which were to make him perhaps the best known motoring artist of all – *The Autocar* in those days having a large circulation. An early example is an Alpine scene dated 1914. A big open Vauxhall, screenless like so many sporting tourers of its day, has stopped to

Artists on rival magazines, Bryan de Grineau of The Motor *(facing page)* and Gordon Crosby of The Autocar *(above) are caught in the characteristic pose of their profession.* Left: *This dramatic Gordon Crosby of a Ballot in the 1922 Targa Florio illustrates the profound influence which Crosby was to exert on the young Geo Ham.* Below left: *Besides working for* The Autocar *Gordon Crosby accepted freelance commissions from private individuals and the industry. This watercolour of a Lagonda saloon at speed dates from 1931.*

admire the Matterhorn.

In addition to his magazine work Crosby seems to have accepted commissions for large pencil and gouache studies of private owners' cars being driven at high speed.

There is no denying the importance of Gordon Crosby and Bryan de Grineau, who have influenced several generations of artists, including many working today. Bryan de Grineau has always suffered by comparison with Gordon Crosby. This may be partly because, although equally sound technically and dramatically, he was less sure as a figure draughtsman; but the main reason, which people seldom realize, is the speed at which de Grineau was required to work. The late pages of *The Motor* went to press on Sunday night so that the magazine, printed on Monday could be on the bookstalls on Tuesday morning. This meant that Bryan would be drawing in the pits while a race was in progress, with a colleague standing over him ready to snatch the pages and drive them to London. Alternatively, drawings would be made after the end of a Sunday race for a belated arrival in London. After about 1930, when *The Motor* chartered an aeroplane for Le Mans, de Grineau would be composing his drawings on the homeward flight as a somewhat draughty bi-plane wallowed in and out of the areas of low-altitude turbulence then known as air pockets.

Crosby by contrast was in clover, as the

rival magazine was not published until Friday. This fact prompted an unkind remark from Laurence Pomeroy, Sr., the Vauxhall designer: 'If you see it in *The Motor* it isn't true. And if you see it in *The Autocar* it isn't news!' Some of Bryan de Grineau's work did suffer from this early deadline, but his reporting of British events, which always took place on Saturday and gave him a little more time, was factual and exciting; it was not his fault if occasionally when several drawings of say a Brooklands race meeting were amalgamated into a single page, the sub-editor sometimes marked them up wrong, so that an M.G. came out larger than a Bentley. These are the hazards of journalism. At his best he was very good, although undervalued and underpaid for his motoring work. Fortunately he had other irons in the

fire: he sold much work to *The Illustrated London News* which paid on a more handsome scale, making cut-away drawings to show the insides of submarines and the like. Another of his jobs was an illustrated History of the World. During the Second World War he was a far-from-chairborne war artist, sending home battle scenes which were some of the best things he ever did. He died in 1957 at the respectable age of seventy-four.

F. Gordon Crosby, like de Grineau, did routine coverage of weekend events. Readers felt hurt if there was no Crosby sketch to show what really happened when some special hit the bank at Shelsley Walsh, or to clarify some incident at Brooklands. The only thing missing from magazines in those days was colour, and this the management proceeded to supply by putting

studio to prove that he knew what the engine of No. 1A looked like; photographic archives at *The Autocar* were remarkably complete. Tyre-changing in those days was as savage as it was simple. As wheels were non-detachable it was necessary to remove the dead tyre and tube. This was done by slashing them through with a knife. Then a new tube and tyre went on and were pumped up to 50 pounds per square inch.

The external complication of those big chain-drive cars with their exposed driving positions and external gear and brake levers invited a restless pencil line, as did the loose road surfaces and the dust thrown up by the cars. After the first war, when Grand Prix regulations shrank the competing cars to a mere 3 litres, then in 1922 to 2 litres, a new sleeker style was required, although roads continued rough for many years, especially when, as often happened, minor races for sports cars or voiturettes were held on the same circuit before the main event. In the new sort of car the cockpit was enclosed and less of the driver and mechanic was visible. The artist had then to win his effects by portraying the light on polished surfaces and on the drama of bouncing axles and wheels. An excellent example of this is Crosby's historical painting of the 1922 French Grand Prix at Strasbourg, when Bugatti was striving to hold off the Fiat challenge. Very boldly the artist shows us the cars from behind, as though they had just passed our observation point beside the long straight tree-lined French road. The drawing conveys an excellent impression of speed, partly by reason of perspective, partly through light. Smoke from the exhaust pipes makes a subtle, attenuated 'speed line' to provide the 'time' dimension, while the car crews act out the excitement of racing and being overtaken. It was a serious loss to illustrators when the riding mechanic was abolished during the mid 1920s.

Crosby was good at people and can usually be counted on to focus attention by means of onlookers in his compositions, as Montaut had often done – a gendarme, a peasant, a group of spectators or a marshal. British participation at Le Mans was a godsend to enthusiasts and illustrators. Thanks to Crosby and his colleagues every corner became familiar territory and the evolution of the circuit could be followed from year to year. The pencil style originating in the days when road circuits were untarred and stony and the surface never lasted a race was very suited to the vehicles

This splendidly Art Deco poster, still bearing the French excise stamps, is an early example of Geo Ham's work, dating from 1927.

Crosby to work on a series of historical paintings leading back from his current output of Grand Prix coverage to races in the fairly remote past. These scenes, issued as a one-page colour supplement from time to time were later collected and sold as portfolios known as *Meteors of Road and Track.*

In these gouache or Conté and wash drawings Crosby set out to recapture the atmosphere, and it is remarkable how well he succeeded in finding the style appropriate to each race and period. He cannot have been present at the first historic encounters and yet there he is, for example, at the 1906 French Grand Prix sketching away while Gabriel and his mechanic change a tyre and, since the bonnet is off, also attend to the works. Perhaps the bonnet was removed by Crosby himself in the

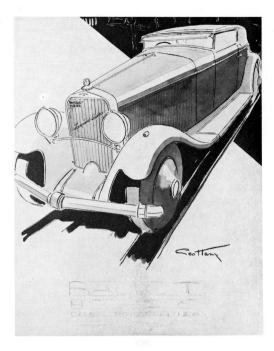

S. C. H. ('Sammy') Davis, besides being sports editor of The Autocar, *drove in many races and record-attempts. In this painting made when he was well into his eighties, he depicts the Aston Martin 'Bunny' on the Brooklands banking. Lionel Martin, the designer, looks on, hands in pockets. Bottom: When Sammy Davis crashed an Invicta in 1930 his colleagues gave him this lively bronze modelled by F. Gordon Crosby.*

of the time, whether rugged Bentley or spidery voiturette. All cars were covered with projections of one sort or another – aero screens inherited from First World War aeroplanes, outside levers for hand-brake and gears, and separate mudguards. The 24 Hours of Le Mans were designed to develop effective road cars, and mud-guards and canvas hoods were compul-sory during the early years. Entrants learned to protect themselves from the stones which flew bulletwise from the car in front. They fitted wire-mesh stoneguards to every vulnerable part – screen, radiator, headlamps, supercharger and fuel tank – and these not only did their own job most of the time but provided the artist with ready-made cross-hatching. Somehow in one's memory of those early Le Mans scenes even the trees, tents and pit-counters have their quota of wire mesh. For Crosby too the multifarious items of pit furniture – petrol churns, quick-lift jacks, spare wheels and copper hammers – all became part of the cast along with mechanics and timekeepers.

The fact that the race went on for twenty-four hours, from four o'clock on Saturday afternoon until four o'clock on Sunday, added greatly to Crosby's repertoire. He became good at lamplit scenes in the pits and at cars racing at night, their headlamps pecking at the road or raking a rival's car on a corner. He was an excellent dramatist, and he certainly made the most of the famous White House crash in 1927.

Breaths are still bated among motoring enthusiasts at memories of that race which shortly after the start gave rise to what is probably the most frequently painted episode in the history of sports car racing – the crash at White House corner which eliminated two out of three Bentleys and damaged the third, which was being dri-ven by S. C. H. Davis, sports editor of *The Autocar*. Let us allow Davis to speak for himself: 'As I swung round that right-hand turn, on the road in front was a scatter of earth, a piece or so of splintered wood, the thing flashed an immediate warning, for I had seen such traces before, in the 1924 Grand Prix, when, round the corner, another car had crashed. Even then it did not occur to me to do more than slow a little and be ready. The car swung round White House corner at almost full speed. I jammed down the brake pedal, tried to spin the wheel, and skidded broadside on, for, white and horrible in the headlights' beam, an appalling tangle of smashed cars appeared right across the road in front! With the rending crash of riven metal we slid right into the mass and brought up all standing with a shock that threw me against the wheel. All the lights went out. . .'

Gingerly, Davis backed the only remain-ing Bentley out of the mess, picked a way through and discovered, at the pits, that the car although bent was still drivable. He and the car's actual owner, Dr. J. D. Ben-jafield, completed the twenty-four hours ahead of all opposition, having covered 1472.4 miles in the time. The first to put this episode on canvas was F. Gordon

Geo Ham turned his hand to everything. On the facing page is a catalogue drawing made when Hispano-Suiza absorbed the Ballot company and produced the hybrid H.S. 26; in the centre, moving on some 20 years, a pencil sketch of a 500 cc Formula III race, and (right) a caricature of the driver/constructor Amédée Gordini.

Crosby, who no doubt used his pencil sketch as the basis of an oil painting which was commissioned by Bentley Motors Ltd. and presented to 'Sammy' Davis as a souvenir of his escape and ultimate victory. This is one of Crosby's best oil paintings. Since then the White House crash has developed into an industry; and first among those who have recorded it must be mentioned Sammy Davis himself. His weekly sporting pages had always been enlivened by amusing little pen and ink drawings, and following his retirement he developed his taste for oil painting. The picture on page 96 showing the $1\frac{1}{2}$-litre side-valve Aston Martin nicknamed 'Bunny' was painted when he was well into his 80s, though it records a drive in which he took part some fifty years before, when the Aston Martin became the first car of less than 1,500 cc to break World records, establishing the best performance recorded irrespective of engine-size.

Pencil, watercolour, gouache, oils, all seemed to come naturally to Gordon Crosby, who was one of the most versatile of artists. Mention of Sammy Davis reminds us that Crosby worked also in three dimensions. When Davis crashed a low-chassis '100 mph' Invicta on Easter Monday at Brooklands in 1930, landing himself in hospital with a broken thigh and other serious injuries, his friends at *The Autocar* presented him with a little Crosby bronze of a contemporary Tourist Trophy racing car inscribed 'To Sammy from his colleagues. Premier award in his greatest trial'. The car is of indeterminate make, a clever synthesis recalling various models

in which or against which Davis had competed in Ulster Tourist Trophy races on the Ards circuit between 1927 and 1929 – Lea-Francis, Alvis, Riley, Aston Martin. The subject is beautifully observed, cornering fast on right lock, the driver watching his inside wheel, which is just lifting, while the mechanic keeps an eye on the dashboard instruments. Enthusiasts would identify the Perrot brakes and note the Ackermann angle of the steering, slightly exaggerated like the fatness of the tyres, for there is a touch of caricature, of artistic idealization, which lifts the work well clear of the model-maker's world, and away from those anonymous but rather endearing bronze or spelter casts of racing cars which had sold well during the Edwardian period. One other Crosby bronze which comes to mind is a plaque, now lost, for the British Racing Drivers' Club in memory of Sir H. R. S. Birkin.

When not illustrating races or painting in oils Gordon Crosby worked away in a pokey little garret at the *Autocar* offices in London on technical illustrations for the magazine. His perspective views of new chassis, or of complete cars with the body 'ghosted' to show the machinery, were most elegant pieces of work. Nor was this his only task at Motor Show time. Every year he would tour the London exhibition with Montague Tombs, the technical editor, making humourous drawings for the light-hearted show report that was an annual feature. He was also an amusing caricaturist, whose work sometimes featured in the sports pages alongside the often very funny idiosyncratic profile

Here surely is René Vincent at his best, capturing the very spirit of French motoring competition during the 1920s – probably near the finish line at the top of the Mont Ventoux hill-climb in Provence. A similar approach is found, applied to a rather different theme in Vincent's poster for Energol oil.

sketches by the sports editor, 'Sammy' Davis, who signed himself Casque.

There is no doubt that Gordon Crosby, like Bryan de Grineau, was consistently undervalued by his employers, although the publication of his *Meteors* and weekly drawings greatly benefited the circulation of their magazine. Gordon Crosby remained with the publishers of *The Autocar*, the Iliffe Press, until the outbreak of war, although increasingly disillusioned. He died tragically in 1942. He remains

every Sunday and racing Bugattis could be bought 'off the peg' and driven on the road without wings. The men who put this on paper were René Vincent, still active into the 1930s, and young Geo Ham, born in 1900 as Georges Hamel, who grew up in the world of cars and aviation. By the time he was twenty-five Geo Ham was drawing extremely stylish catalogue illustrations – though it is doubtful whether he received very much for them from a small manufacturer like Benjamin. The Autodrome de Linas-Montlhéry had just been opened, forming a headquarters for everyone interested in speed within a few minutes drive from Paris, and Geo Ham was very much of this circle. Perhaps there have never been more professional drawings of racing cars than those he produced in the 1920s, if by professional we mean drawings from the viewpoint of the racing driver. To own a Bugatti at that time was every young Frenchman's ambition and if Geo Ham did not yet own one he certainly knew how to drive. Like 'John A. Bryan' and Ernest Ford he took his public into the cockpit, but not now as mere passengers: Geo Ham himself sat in the driver's seat and his was the view he drew. Nothing could be more atmospheric than his pencil sketch of the cockpit of a Type 35 – except the watercolour he worked up from it. One can smell the castor oil, hear the sound of tearing calico and feel the front wheels kick as his gloved hands steady the corded rim of the steering wheel. Another Bugatti is in front and a pale blue Delage has just passed – Robert Benoist perhaps, or René Thomas of steering-wheel fame, or Albert Divo, three members of the Delage championship team. Never since those days of two-seater bodies and open cockpits have cars been so graphogenic.

Geo Ham, in short, was as French as Crosby and de Grineau were English. By 1928 he had reached the top of the tree. He was drawing covers for *L'Illustration*, the Frenchman's window on the world, taken in all the best houses, on tap in all the best bars: the magazine of magazines when magazines were the equivalent of television. As befitted an enthusiast Geo Ham invented imaginary cars and no schoolboy ever drew them with more zest. We find these entrancing mock-ups on the covers of magazines and in his illustrations to stories. He also turned them to account when designing posters. One especially effective design seems to be viewed from some dug-out in the road. We sit securely below the surface while a single-seater rushes less than a yard away – a device

however the most versatile and most popular British artist of his kind. Thanks to him and Bryan de Grineau we have a complete portfolio of cars and racing personalities stretching all the way from 1914 until 1939; we still look at racing, especially Vintage racing, through their eyes.

British enthusiasts during the period when those artists were working looked longingly toward France, where fast motoring was *snob* rather than clandestine, where there was a race or a hill-climb

Facing page: Autoportrait, *oil on wood by Tamara de Lempicka, was painted for the cover of* Die Dame *during the mid-1920s: an arresting glimpse of the liberated* Sportlerin *in the days of the Weimar Republic.*

René Vincent in the early 1930s patriotically invokes the Tricolore in presenting a new Chenard et Walker. He died in 1936.

borrowed perhaps from René Vincent. All we see is one half of the car in exaggerated perspective and the concentrated face of its driver, one hand on an outside gear-lever. The car is imaginary but it is in the style of American track racers and was no doubt inspired by the Derby-Miller in which Mrs. Gwenda Stewart held the lap-record at Montlhéry. Ham worked often in this manner, for races at the French track; there was hardly a fixture in France that did not at some time commission a poster by Geo Ham. His style could also be quiet and poetic, as witness a poster for the sand races at La Baule. Nor was his popularity surprising, for he was truly *sportif*, as much at home in the air as in the driver's seat. He was for instance one of only five artists accredited to the Ministry for Air, and he was on the staff of *La Vie Aérienne*, and of *L'Illustration*, from 1927 to 1940,

during which time he flew with all the great pilots of L'Aéropostale while that French airline was opening up the South American routes, including Jean Mermoz and Antoine de Saint-Exupéry. He also covered the Ethiopian War as war correspondent and was recommended for the Croix de Guerre. During 1939–1940 he served as a driver and was mentioned in dispatches.

Often especially in his later work, the paintings for Roger Labric's first volume of Le Mans history and for the Golden Jubilee celebrations of the Automobile Club de l'Ouest, one sees how strongly Geo Ham was influenced by Gordon Crosby, especially when working against the clock. But his own individual poster style has many followers still. Béligond, for example, although no copyist, has evidently admired Geo Ham. Ham himself had many styles, and it would be unfair to leave him without a thought for the delightful little pencil sketch he made of Amedée Bollée's steam coach – an historical exercise probably for his own amusement.

During his years on *L'Illustration* and no doubt in La Potinière, the café-restaurant at Montlhéry where drivers used to meet, Geo Ham would have seen a lot of René Vincent, who was still at the height of his powers. Perhaps the best racing picture Vincent ever painted was his watercolour of a beautiful blue single-seater, the epitome of French motoring sport during the 1920s, bounding into the clouds above, perhaps, Mont Ventoux. René Vincent continued drawing and painting during the 1930s, and was responsible for some very striking publicity work, including catalogues for Michelin and posters for Citroën and Chenard et Walcker which brim with imagination. He was also in demand as an illustrator of stories written by himself in various periodicals, including *L'Illustration* and *The Englebert Magazine*, a rather amusing monthly put out by the Belgian tyre company. Throughout his long career René Vincent inspired many artists, and one seems to find echoes of his later manner in the work of Guy Sabran, another *L'Illustration* man, who celebrated the world of concours d'élégance during their hey-day of the early 1930s. As a complete contrast to the amateurs' world of the British, the elegance of Vincent and Ham, let us close this chapter with a plate from *Die Dame*, an 'autoportrait' by Tamara de Lempicka which personifies the Teutonic challenge – tough, blonde, soignée and decadent, her jackboot crushing the throttle.

Art for Enthusiasts 2

Roy Nockolds, Peter Helck and others

WHILE SPORTS CAR RACING, Brooklands and Montlhéry continued non-stop throughout the late 1920s, and 1930s, creating and maintaining their own styles of drawing, Grand Prix racing changed radically with the abandonment of the riding mechanic after 1926, although Bugatti and others went on making two-seater cars with the private customer in mind. Road surfaces also improved, chain drive had long since disappeared, and exhausts were cleaner thanks to better fuels and oils, so that artists were deprived of their old ally 'pork'. New styles were therefore evolved to handle the new situation.

By their very splendour and complication the 1½-litre straight-eight Delages of 1927 frightened away official opposition. Racing became a free-for-all, with sporting Bugattis and Alfa Romeos competing in *formule libre.* Then despite the financial slump came the era of twin-cam Bugattis, and the *monoposto* Alfa and Maserati: relatively tall, extremely slim and graceful motorcars which pleaded to be drawn in a new way. New men were ready. In England Roy Nockolds had been drawing since he was a young schoolboy in the 1920s. He made dry-point engravings of the great drivers for Bugatti, Alfa Romeo and Maserati at full chat. Each driver had his characteristic attitude in the open cockpit, instantly recognizable at a distance, and cornering styles were individu-

al. No-one could mistake the suave classic line taken by Achille Varzi, a stylist in the tradition of Felice Nazzaro, nor the dramatic improvizations of Tazio Nuvolari, who knew all the rules but re-wrote them as he went along. These attitudes and methods were deftly captured by the early Roy Nockolds, who allowed both cars and the drivers to act. So great was the rivalry between these two men that Enzo Ferrari who was then in charge of Alfa Romeo's racing programme would not have them both on his team. 'You don't', he remarked, 'have two cocks in one henroost!' The effect of ten more years' racing on the faces of these two great professionals is shown by the excellent Rudy Zeeman portraits on page 104. All too few portraits of racing drivers survive. Their timetable hardly encourages sittings, so we tend to be left with photographs and caricatures.

As conditions relaxed after the financial depression of the early 1930s new magazines started up and new racing teams appeared in the field. Germany, long cold-shouldered by international organizers, had not neglected her own motor racing; Mercedes had been active since the very early 1920s, Benz had built a rear-engined racing car which showed the shape of things to come, and as part of a programme to relieve unemployment two important circuits had been built, the AVUS in Berlin (now bisected by the Wall)

Right: *Portraits of racing drivers, other than hack work and caricature, are very rare. These drawings by Rudy Zeeman appeared in* The Motor *in 1938 when those two great drivers Varzi the stylist and Nuvolari the innovator were still battling after ten years of intense rivalry. Zeeman here has affinities with the German Expressionists, particularly in the portrait of Varzi, whose private life was shadowed and intense at that time.*

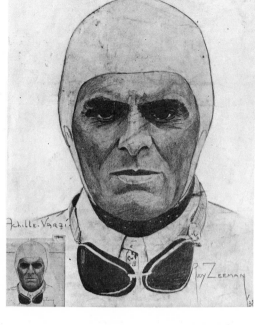

and the Nürburgring in the Eifel Mountains. Even before the Nazis came to power a private syndicate (with partly Jewish backing) had been formed to race rear-engined cars designed by Dr. Ferdinand Porsche, and Mercedes, tired of their monstrous SSKL ex-sports cars, had new single-seaters ready. The appearance of both these teams in 1934 as rivals to Bugatti, Maserati and Alfa Romeo gave tremendous impetus to racing and demanded new artistic techniques, since the German cars were silver in colour (with red numbers) and less heraldic in outline than the machines of the Vintage years. The great power of these cars of the '750-kilo' Formula (which imposed a maximum dry weight of 15 cwt without wheels and tyres) brought new cornering methods. Instead of being guided round by the steering or power-slid on opposite lock like dirt-track machines, they cornered in what was known as a 'four-wheel drift': front wheels turned in towards the apex and the car held in this attitude by the power fed to the back wheels. These methods were eagerly studied in photographs by Louis Klemantaski and George Monkhouse, the best camera men of the time; and by no-one more avidly than Monkhouse's close friend, Richard Seaman, the English driver on the Mercedes team, who won the German Grand Prix in 1938.

The '750-kilo' cars were faster than ever before, touching 180 mph on the straight and exceeding 200 mph at the AVUS circuit in record-breaking form. They also had no more colour than a fish, save that which they picked up from their surroundings. Roy Nockolds therefore revived Impressionist techniques, while retaining the natural outline required by his subjects and public. Light became all-important, the blue and purple of sky reflected in roads, the dappled shadows at wooded circuits like the Bremgarten in Berne, the golden scatter from the cornfields at Rheims where cars reached some of the highest speeds. Heat was also a factor; the best of Nockolds shimmers with speed and sun while never ignoring the driver's 'line' whether on the straight or holding a drift. My favourite amongst pre-war Nockolds oil paintings shows Dick Seaman in green linen helmet at the wheel of a 3-litre Mercedes-Benz of the type in which he won the German Grand Prix at the Nürburgring in 1938.

Roy Nockolds specialized in movement, cars at speed rather than in the pits. But the pits were exceedingly busy, as races were long (300 miles) fuel consumption heavy and tyres very expendable, except for those on the cars of Seaman and Caracciola whose wonderful 'hands' made them last. Pit-scenes were meat and drink to the illustrators and have proved so since to re-creators of the period, of whom the German Hans Liska especially springs to mind from the 1950s, and Walter Gotschke of today. Roy Nockolds maintained his interest in speed well into the post-war seasons; and one of his most memorable canvases shows the duel among the cornfields of Rheims when Fangio's Maserati and Mike Hawthorn's Ferrari were racing wheel-to-wheel in 1958. The light, the shimmer and the evanescence of speed are all there.

Left: *Roy Nockolds is the best known of contemporary English motoring artists. The painting of Achille Varzi in the 1931 Targa Florio, (in which he came third driving an 'unofficial' works Bugatti) clearly owes much in mood and style to Gordon Crosby; but in the picture below Nockolds has found a style all his own. This painting of Richard Seaman winning the 1938 German Grand Prix is Roy Nockolds's masterpiece: a brilliant Impressionist study of a smooth car at very high speed on a smooth road.*

Previous pages: *A Roy Nockolds study of Vintage machinery in the 1921 French Grand Prix on a circuit at Le Mans: a very historic event in which Jimmy Murphy (Duesenberg) became the first, and so far unique, American driver to win a Continental G.P. in an American car. Behind him, Ralph DePalma, another American, in a French straight-eight Ballot. Right: In this miracle of complexity L. C. Cresswell lucidly unravels the mechanism of the 16-cylinder B.R.M. for readers of* The Motor. *The Scuderia Ferrari i.f.s. monoposto Alfa Romeo drawing below was contributed by a very youthful Russell Brockbank to the monthly* Speed, *official organ of the British Racing Drivers' Club.*

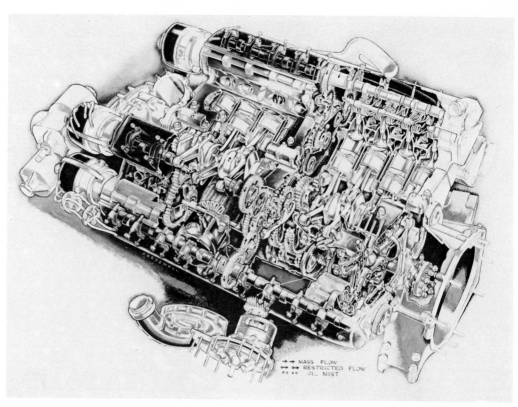

→ → MASS FLOW
⊷ ⊷ RESTRICTED FLOW
∘∘ ∘∘ OIL MIST

Today Nockolds tends to specialize in what may be called automobile genre paintings – portraits of clients' favourite, usually antique, cars in a picturesque setting, and re-creations of historic encounters.

The early Nockolds first appeared in *The Autocar, The Motor* and *Motor Sport*. Mention of the last-named monthly is a reminder that *Speed*, which flourished as the official organ of the British Racing Drivers' Club from 1935 until 1939, when it was absorbed by *Motor Sport*, made the name of several artists. Their staff illustrator was H. J. Moser, who, when not bedevilled by deadlines and pork was a good graphic black-and-white man, especially good at headings. Back numbers of *Speed* also introduce a name which became very well known indeed. Scraperboard drawings of racing cars – an R-type M.G. being pushed in the paddock, an Alfa held with its inside front wheel brushing the kerb on a tight corner – draw attention to the keen observation of a very young artist signing himself R. P. Brockbank, later known simply as Brockbank. Russell Brockbank himself is inclined to dismiss his early racing drawings, but one is forced to disagree. He is probably the only man who ever drew an E.R.A. as it should be drawn, with just that element of caricature that makes a likeness stick. During the war Brockbank served in the Royal Canadian Navy, and sent home from every imaginable station cartoons of motor cars and aeroplanes which have never been excelled. After the war his comic drawings and weekly strip showing the adventures of 'Major Upset' were a weekly feature of *The Motor* – and *Motor*; he also became art editor of *Punch*.

Other artists published in early issues of *Speed* were Angus Stewart (pencil) and Rex Hunt. They also ran a competition for young motor racing artists, and it is interesting to find amongst these two whose prints and drawings have enjoyed a fol-

R P BROCKBANK '35

lowing ever since. They were Norman Edward Giles (who later signed 'Drawn by Giles') and Michael L. Wright, both of whom seemed to enjoy very much the racing of the 1930s, especially the round-the-houses G.P. at Monte Carlo. The *Speed* competition was won by Norman Giles then aged 18, while Michael Wright found his name in the same paper at 15.

Besides Crosby and occasionally Brockbank, *The Motor* in pre-war days carried amusing drawings by Gordon Wilkins, whose drawings were as good as his general reporting but unpaid by an unappreciative management so that he stopped doing them, which was a pity. There was also an entertaining Ulsterman named Nevin who once signed a drawing 'Nevinsky' on the ground that only foreign artists grew famous and has been known to many as Nevinsky ever since. They also had a very good all-round commercial artist passionately devoted to cars named George Lane. George, unfit for the armed forces, spent an adventurous war in the Auxiliary Fire Service. During the war *The Motor* kept the blood circulating by means of historical articles, and here George Lane proved invaluable, being seemingly at home in any period. He could always be relied upon for a lively set of drawings and his cars always behaved like cars. Historical racing articles were popular, and even more so was the series 'Milestones of Speed' in which Laurence Pomeroy, the technical editor (son of L. H. Pomeroy the designer), delved into the history of racing car design with that wonderful technical draughtsman, L. C. Cresswell.

The ploy, for Pomeroy's *Milestones of Speed* series was to analyze, down to the last nut and bolt, such historically significant racing cars as were to be found within reach of London, and assign them with all

possible facts, figures and deductions to their place on the graph of progress. With a long war in prospect Leslie Cresswell had the opportunity to indulge himself as never before, and as the months went by there came from his drawing-board a series of superb cut-away drawings, each one

from a different aspect and presented not merely as a double-page spread, but as a plate in the book which Pomeroy and the publishers already had in mind. This book appeared after the war, with additional material, as *The Grand Prix Car 1906–1939*. Probably the only man alive who could have rivalled Cresswell in this matter was Max Millar, his opposite number on *The Autocar*, and fortunately for Temple Press 'the opposition' possessed no Laurence Pomeroy.

Motoring history on such a scale had never been attempted before. These articles and others dealing with great drivers and races were eagerly seized upon by

enthusiasts as a substitute for the real thing. Through subscribers in the Navy, Army and Air Force they whetted appetites all over the world. The monthly *Motor Sport* also blew upon the members.

Suddenly, when the war stopped, history-painting became a growth industry in the United States, in Britain, France, Italy and Germany. Nockolds and Geo Ham reviewed races they had seen. Conte Carlo Biscaretti di Ruffia revisited the collection of historic vehicles stored beneath the seats of Turin's municipal stadium, machines he had saved from destruction by purchase when he was the only collector in the field, including racing cars which the Fiat directors had been anxious to throw away. It was Biscaretti's ambition to form a public museum, and this he succeeded in doing in the final years of a long

Below left: This later Brockbank cartoon, from the period in which the artist signed his work with his surname only, speaks for itself. Left: 'That's Shell that was!' was perhaps the most famous slogan of its day. This original drawing by Rex Whistler (1905–1944), brother of Laurence Whistler the poet and glass engraver (see page 141) hangs in the chairman's office in Shell Mex House in London. Rex Whistler made many sports car drawings for his own amusement, besides rediscovering the gaieties of Baroque decoration. He was killed in action during the commando raid on Dieppe in the Second World War. Below: 'Fougasse' (Cyril Kenneth Bird, 1888–1965), most economical of draughtsmen, drew many motoring jokes, including a hilarious set of 'annotations' to the Highway Code. He worked mainly for Punch, *of which weekly he became art editor.*

'I wonder if it's cured that squeak.'

life; the Biscaretti Motor Museum, now in sumptuous new premises at Turin, is a memorial to his enthusiasm. He died shortly before the opening, but during the last few years of his life he had been busy recording history in an unending series of charming watercolours concerning the motoring past. Draughtsmanship had been his hobby and occasionally his profession: he designed the Lancia badge – a lance and flag, *lancia* being Italian for lance – and he also made delicate drawings for the parts lists of Lancia, Olivetti and others. Having been in the industry all his life, and having ridden his first race (on a motor tricycle) before the turn of the century, he knew all there was to be known about Italian cars, motor racing and drivers. It is not surprising therefore that some of his re-creations are often taken for contemporary work.

In America the best-known history-painter is undoubtedly Peter Helck. His work is vivid, thronged with spectatorial life and rooted in the American tradition,

Count Carlo Biscaretti di Ruffia, artist, pioneer racing driver and son of one of the founders of Fiat, collected old cars during the 1920s and 1930s when he was almost alone in the field. His personal collection formed the basis of the great Museum at Turin which forms his monument (below, left). The Count's historical watercolours combine accuracy with charm. In the example shown here, Victor Hémery on a Darracq 200 h.p. sets a new world speed record of 110.30 mph on 30th December 1905. Biscaretti also made many 'exploded' mechanical drawings for catalogues and spare-parts lists, and was the designer of the Lancia badge (below, right).

carefully researched. Among his treasured possessions is a huge 90 horsepower Locomobile racing car 'Number Sixteen' dating from the Vanderbilt Cup races of 1906, when it was driven in the American Eliminating race by Helck's friend and neighbour Joe Tracy. Tracy rode as mechanic to George Robertson in the same car when it won the 1908 Vanderbilt.

Correspondence with Peter Helck in connexion with this book revealed him as an artist of amazing versatility. He seems just as much at home with Taruffi's win for Lancia in the 1954 Targa Florio and the Moss/Jenkinson Mille Miglia of 1955 as with the great races at the turn of the century and the opening of the Indianapolis Speedway. His memory goes back a long way and he has evidently seen many races. The fact that he studied painting in London under the great muralist and designer Sir Frank Brangwyn, R.A., helps to explain the rhythm of his compositions and the unerringly decorative backgrounds, which always situate his paintings in time and space. In a brief autobiographical note posted in January 1978, Helck starts by paying tribute to E. Montaut. 'I am sure', he writes, 'my first encounter with Montaut's prints about 1905 initiated my own interest in a sport so rich in pictorial possibilities.

'Other factors were rides given to a small boy in Simplex stripped racing chassis and race cars by tester Al Poole. This Coventry-born lad had been C. S. Rolls's mechanic on the former's Panhard in England's Thousand Miles Trial in 1900. My acquaintance with Poole accounted for my witnessing my first auto race, the 1906 Vanderbilt Cup. Seeing my friend, mechanic Al Poole aboard Joe Tracy's Locomobile hitting a hundred along North Hempstead Turnpike clinched my obsession with racing. That same day provided another memorable treat. An hour after Louis Wagner's win he was driving his Darracq to its racing headquarters. I was lunching with relatives, heard the approaching exhaust, rushed to the porch in time to wave to the dashing driver. Wagner returned my salute! Forty years on I sent

Doyen of U.S. car painters, Peter Helck, N.A. of Millerton, New York, saw his first motor race in 1906 and has remained enthusiastic ever since. He studied in London under the great muralist Sir Frank Brangwyn, R.A., which may account for the decorative qualities of his work and the lucid marshalling of facts. Helck acknowledges his debt to Brangwyn, to Montaut and to Crosby but his style is very much his own, making dramatic use of spectators as well as the competing vehicles. Top left: Ed Pullen's Mercer during the 1914 American Grand Prize, when he gave America her first win in this annual classic. Collection Robert V. Trainer. Top right: On a wet road with Lancia (Fiat No. 4) out, Théry goes on to win the 1905 Gordon Bennett Trophy. Collection Hal Clark. Bottom picture: George Robertson's Locomobile, the winner, leading Haupt's Chadwick in the 1908 Vanderbilt Cup on Long Island. Locomobile No. 16 now belongs to Peter Helck, who has known it all its life. Collection Lawrence Greenwald.

him a sketch of this incident. We became pen pals which led to our congenial meetings at his home in Montlhéry.

'Though most of my work from 1912 was related to the heavy industries: railroading, steel production etc., my play-time was given to depicting fire-snorting chain-driven monsters. My first professional assignment in this vein were program covers for the Brighton Motordrome, 1913, then for the super Sheepshead Speedway, 1915–1916. During 1920–1921 I was a private student under that truly great master, Frank Brangwyn, in Hammersmith, London. Obviously Brooklands beckoned. I'll never forget my first view of this fabulous race course, seemingly capable of housing several Indy Speedways!

'I covered several meets there for *Autocar* for which I'm forever grateful to its then editor, Geoffrey Smith. While so engaged I passed the time of day with Malcolm Campbell, Frank Clement, Le Champion and lesser lights, and was given a few snappy laps around Weybridge's rough circuit with Miss Ivy Cummings aboard her 30-98 Vauxhall.

'Always present was the wish to meet Gordon Crosby whose work had – and still has – my complete admiration. But I simply lacked the courage to initiate this into realization. Besides, I was told that he was in poor health.

'Supplementing my studies under Brangwyn were racing and non-racing covers and advertising paintings for Morris, Packard, Noma, etc. Back in U.S.A. I did some racing subjects for Veedol, Champion Spark Plugs and posters for the 1936–1937 Vanderbilt Cup revivals at the ultra modern Roosevelt Raceway. But the first opportunity to portray racing's appeal was the series of eight full-color spreads for *Esquire*, 1944–1945. Shortly after this came assignments for *True*, of which the most enjoyable was a painting to illustrate dear old Gerald Rose's [Author of *A Record of Motor Racing*, London 1909], review of the 1908 A.C.F. Grand Prix. . . .'

Following publication of his first book *The Checkered Flag* (Scribner's 1961) Peter Helck has worked mainly on private

Below: The pit-work paraphernalia add excitement to this re-creation by Terence Cuneo of Bentley days at Le Mans. In the 1929 24 Hours race the 4½ litre of Jack Dunfee and Glen Kidston, hotly pursued by Chrysler No. 14 driven by Henri Stoffel and Robert Benoist, passes while Dr. Benjafield tops up with oil.

Above: *Robertson's Simplex, winner of the 318-mile Lowell Trophy road race in 1909, leans excitedly forward in this painting by Peter Helck, who borrows a trick from press photographs taken with the focal-plane shutter. Collection Rick Carroll. Bottom, left: Hémery (Darracq voiturette) blocks Heath (Panhard) in the 1905 Vanderbilt Cup. Collection Charles W. Bishop. Bottom, right: A treatment by Peter Helck of the bridge at Eu during the 1908 French Grand Prix. The victor, Lautenschlager (Mercedes), leads Felice Nazzaro (Fiat). Collection George H. Waterman, Jr.*

commissions for individuals and museums. His latest book, *Great Auto Races* (Harry N. Abrams, 1976), 'discloses', he says 'to what degree my obsession prevails.'

Scenes of pit and paddock, start and finish have always appealed to draughtsmen equally trained in cars and figures. One notices this not only in Helck but in the work of Hans Liska, whose evocations of Mercedes and Benz history were put to good use by the combined company in the early 1950s in several publicity portfolios, and of another German artist, Walter Gotschke, who has illustrated much historical work in the U.S. magazine *Automobile Quarterly*. The same is true in Britain of Terence Cuneo. A drawing by him of pit work during the 1912 French

Grand Prix showing David Bruce Brown's Fiat and one of the Sunbeams was recently reproduced by an Italian publication, in an article on motoring art. The driver holds a large funnel while a mechanic directs petrol into it from a large-diameter hose; big jacks stand ready for a possible wheel-change and there is a tall red churn labelled EAU. Beyond on the sandy road Georges Boillot's 'little' 7.6-litre Peugeot raises the dust as it overtakes Bruce Brown's 14.1-litre Fiat, last of the racing monsters. A shimmer of heat rises from the standing Sunbeam. Good stirring stuff with dramatic shadows and lots of action. This piece of pastiche succeeded so well that the Italian caption-writer mistook it for a genuine contemporary painting: 'The acme of Art Nouveau. This picture by

Cuneo, laden with excitement, was often to inspire Achille Beltrame.' The caption-writer got the date wrong and Beltrame, unlike Cuneo, was working before the Great War; but the painting is an authentic evocation of the past, and convincing to students of history. Cuneo works from contemporary photographs and also whenever possible from study of actual vehicles. A painting in his autobiography *The Mouse and its Master* (New Cavendish Books, London, 1975) shows Woolf Barnato beating the Blue Train from Paris to Nice in his Bentley. The actual Gurney Nutting Speed Six coupé survives and the drawing was based on this, altered where necessary to retrace the march of time.

Besides Cuneo, present-day British artists include Michael Turner whose black and white drawings I prefer to his oil paintings. The emphasis now is on the past, perhaps because a nostalgia public exists, and perhaps also because the modern Grand Prix car, with its dazzle-painting of advertisement and aerofoil paraphernalia seems to have mislaid its outline. For this reason Frank Wootton when working for *Motor* migrated from racing to rallies, where mud, stones, and headlamp beams made things more picturesque. His work was always vivid and exciting. Unfortunately he has deserted motor reporting for other, often equine, fields of artistic endeavour.

Surprisingly few new approaches have been explored, considering the vitality of painting in the world sense, now that artists have shaken off the fetters of abstract-

Above: *Terence Cuneo shows a side-valve 3-litre Sunbeam at the pits on its way to winning the 1912 Coupe de l'Auto and finishing third in the French G.P. which was run concurrently. First and second respectively in the G.P. were Georges Boillot (Peugeot No. 22) and Louis Wagner (Fiat No. 37). The period flavour has been so well caught by Cuneo that this painting was recently described by an Italian writer as an excellent piece of Art Nouveau, very typical of its period.*

115

Right: *The German artist Hans Liska made several albums or sketch-books as publicity for Mercedes-Benz during the early 1950s.* Facing page, right: *Dexter Brown, working in England during the 1960s, was beguiled by the play of light on surfaces; his work, although not 'photographic' in the naturalistic sense, does suggest a world of cars seen via colour transparencies. The upper picture is a montage for a poster design, the lower shows Denny Hulme in a McLaren M8D.*

Today's market for racing pictures is two-fold: the historical and the recent, a point made by these two works. Right: *Michael Wright, who as a schoolboy saw his work published in* Speed *as long ago as 1935, clearly shows Crosby and Nockolds influences in this evocation of Varzi's Bugatti in the 1931 Targa Florio.* Facing page: *Michael Turner may well be drawing from memory. The cars from the German G.P. at the Nürburgring 1972 are Jackie Ickx's Ferrari which won, and the March of Ronnie Peterson on the Adenau bridge. Aerofoils and suspension struts have brought back some of the complication lacking from the cars of the late thirties.*

ion and started to explore the figurative with new eyes. Pop Art and Hyper Realism will be discussed in a later chapter. Meanwhile other photographic influences have been at work. We have seen how early draughtsmen adopted the distortions of the focal-plane shutter in order to represent speed. Today it is not distortion but light itself that has been the influence, by the way of colour transparencies. Perhaps the first to be beguiled by the bright colours and twinkling high-lights of this medium was the young painter Dexter Brown in the early 1960s; his dragster paintings from this period shimmer and vibrate with suppressed motion. Perhaps similar forces have influenced the Italian Raymond Moretti, whose work pays homage to his Futurist compatriots Giacomo Balla, Gino Severini and Luigi Russolo. It is evident that many new directions remain to be explored in the depiction of speed, which will remain a challenge so long as motor racing exists.

Pop Art to Photo Realism

The car in contemporary painting and sculpture

TODAY MORE INTERNATIONAL EXHIBITORS are painting cars than ever before. Suddenly in the 1960s motor cars, and very recognizable motor cars at that, started finding their way into the work of the avant-garde. 'Realer than real', they appear in landscape, in genre, in life and in death; optimistic, pessimistic, touring, racing, technical and poetic – no longer left to enthusiasts, illustrators and poster men but an object for exploration – which is what art, like poetry, is all about.

Oddly enough these explorations have not been due to artists especially keen on the subject. Early masters like Bonnard, Max Jacob, Jules Forain and keen drivers like André Derain, Kees van Dongen, Matisse, despite an occasional carscape, quickly became busy elsewhere. Fernand Léger distilled what he wanted from machines and passed along; the Futurists wove fantasies of speed but not of the car itself. Surrealists on the whole took a gloomy glance at the motoring scene, and academic artists approached it without much understanding. But now we have close-ups of racing engines, canvases six feet by eight celebrating the car, putting tremendous sparkle back into the motoring scene. For the first time in history the shape, the texture, the sheer lustre of automobiles have got serious artists excited. And never before have so many different media been employed. Let us make a short

list: pencil; watercolour; oils; acrylic. Now another short list: brush, air brush; spray gun; masking tape; welding-torch; and multi-ton hydraulic press. A far cry indeed from the old Edwardian standbys of allegory, 'pork' and dust.

Two revolutions were mainly responsible, namely Pop Art and what here will be called Photo Realism, both movements of the last twenty years. There are signs already of newer, even more exciting developments that are only to be expected as everyday cars become banal, racing cars discover new shapes and new artists' materials appear. Let us hope that young artists today will be treated understandingly by art critics and the people interested in cars. They should not expect great understanding from their own immediate elders, because it seems almost a law of nature for new work to be dismissed by the very people to whom it might be expected to appeal. When Matisse's *Joie de Vivre*, one of the seminal Post-Impressionist paintings, scandalized people in 1906, we are told by Linda Chase (*Photo Realism*, Eminent Publications, New York, 1975), 'the angriest of all was Paul Signac. A modern painter and member of the avant-garde himself, he nevertheless asserted that Matisse had "gone to the dogs". . . But only a year later Matisse attacked Picasso's new painting *Les Demoiselles d'Avignon*, calling it an outrage and claiming that Picasso

includes cars depicted with almost figurative fidelity and the same is true of another eminent British painter, Professor Carel Weight, whose *Wandsorth Stadium*, painted some twenty years later, has cars which are recognizable as to make but freely and pictorially treated. The United States, which might have been expected from its enormous car population to have many paintings to show, seems, in fact, to have few apart from magazine illustrations. The Social Realist Aaron Bohrod's *Landscape near Chicago* (1934), showing a rather weary tourer outside a prairie farmhouse, is one of the few that come to mind – a perfect counterpart to John Steinbeck's *The Grapes of Wrath*. Perhaps some reader will happen upon a Stuart Davis in which this latter-day Léger finds room for motor imagery amongst his pre-Pop compositions of packages, lettering and everyday objects.

An influx of European avant-garde painters before and during the Second World War rescued America from the provincialism that had largely prevailed during the Depression and the Federal efforts to overcome it. New York became the home of Abstraction on the grandest and most exuberant scale. Individual sensibility, then Action Painting – the free use of paint for its own sake – ruled out figurative, representational art and became the sort of art

had painted it to ridicule the modern movement.' On a motoring plane of course the same thing happened to Dr. Porsche's 'wind-cheating' Austro-Daimlers in 1910, also to rear- and mid-engined racing cars, and the first cars to wear aerofoils in racing. The same thunderings greeted Pop and Photo Realism. But first we take a look at some hardy or reactionary souls who had kept a form of realism alive during the years of Abstract art. We have already spoken of Robert Bevan and Charles Ginner in connexion with the Camden Town Group before 1914, and it is not entirely unfair to mention Dame Laura Knight (1877–1970) in the same breath, for her *Derby Day* of 1932 in the Barron Collection

Above: *Dame Laura Knight, R.A., was one of the few Royal Academicians to attempt cars in her paintings. The result in* Derby Day, *here, is either too much naturalism or not enough.* Right: *Primitive influences, and the provincial Social Realism bred by the U.S. Federal Relief Project's job-creation scheme are alike evident in* Landscape near Chicago *(1934) by Aaron Bohrod, now in the Whitney Museum of American Art, N.Y.*

taught in the schools. Nothing could be more commonplace, figurative and philistine than that mere consumer-durable, a car. Picasso perhaps summed this up in a sculpture, *Baboon and Young* (1951), now in the Norman Grantz Collection. In this bronze, part modelling, part *objets trouvés*, he forms a toy Renault into the cranium of an ape; and nothing could be more low-brow than that. Strange to think that during the very same years Picasso's old companion from the *bateau lavoir* days, Maurice Vlaminck, Fauve traditions now forgotten, was still painting landscapes of the open road, preferably snow-covered, mentally controlling wheelspin in his Bugatti. Houses lean outwards as the car rushes on, the familiar willows sway beside gloomy little garages. Here are some of the dates and titles of Vlamincks one would like to find: *Neige*, 1932; *Route Enneigée*, 1935; *La RN 30* and *La Nationale*, 1953; and two dramatic scenes painted by the light of headlamps in the same period: *Phares* and *Cercottes, la Nuit*.

America too had painters of the road. An artist who was among the first to isolate the motorized quality of America was Edward Hopper (born 1882, two years after Picas-

so), a wilfully old-fashioned realist in a world of abstraction. Hopper though an interesting painter is the high-priest of boredom – and hence a precursor of Pop. His characters sit or stand around mutely in the certainty that nothing will turn up. One thinks of the usherette in his *New York Movie* of 1939, his café full of *Nighthawks* in the small hours, but most of all of a painting called *Gas*. A country roadside pull-up with its little row of pumps under a lowering sky: a station where no-one goes except customers, every customer a non-event.

Just when American Abstract Expressionism, the New York School, was at the height of its international prestige, New York was rocked by a series of one-man shows by Roy Lichtenstein, James Rosenquist, Andy Warhol, Tom Wesselmann and Robert Indiana. The work of these men twanged automobiles back into the art galleries. It was also blasphemy in the grand manner, not because it blasphemed against God but because it blasphemed the new opium of the people, newspapers and television. Newspapers have always found cars an image of violence, an excuse for the daily ration of 'grue'. For years they

Top: *Edward Hopper more than any other painter put loneliness into his pictures.* Gas *(1940) was unusual in having a rural setting and artificial light. Some artists avoid cars as a 'lowbrow' subject.* Bottom: *Picasso went further than that: he used a car as the brain-pan of an ape.*

121

Right: *Having worked for years as a billboard-painter, James Rosenquist paints on a very large scale.* Silver Skies *(1962), an early and typical assemblage of Pop Art imagery, measures 6 ft 6 in. by 18 ft 6 in. The later painting* 'Ultra-Violet Cars' *(1966), on the facing page, has elements of realism almost totally abstracted.*

plugged accident statistics, licking their lips when casualties rose, keeping silent when they fell. Television has brought violence more intimately into the home; the macabre fantasy-realities of Warhol, the insupportable mixture of blood and iron that the Czech Franta has made his own. The mindlessness of the media, the existential presentation of the good, the bad and the bland – the acceptance of these standards as reality became due to be mocked.

To say in 1960 'We don't have television' was infinitely more shocking than 'I'm afraid we don't go to church', and the new artists found a style that hit the great public where it lived. The new art, quickly christened Pop, was realistic too in a harsh, brash, vulgar, one-thousand per-cent American way, and could not therefore be Art which, it was now well known, must be abstract, painterly, and thoroughly incomprehensible.

Selecting the most blatant, vulgar, worthless and ephemeral elements in the American environment, the new Pop artists made people realize they had been accepting nothing for something. They had lost their sense of scale and their sense of values. The public had to look again and this made them cross. Pop Art was doing what René Magritte did with his pipe labelled 'This is not a pipe'. It wasn't, of course; it was a painting of a pipe. No-one understood this better than James Rosenquist, who had spent seven formative years as a billboard painter: 'I was a real worker. They'd say "O.K., James, you're going out to the Mayfair Theater to paint a boy and a dog 75 feet long".' He would then climb out of a tenth storey window and set to work. This somewhat naturally made him more interested in the perception of objects than in the objects themselves. The technical problems of painting the highlight on a dog's nose three-feet wide were to interest him when he came to paint close-ups of auto panels. Rosenquist knew the value of enlarged detail. When the television camera at a concert homes in on a player's left nostril it gives a new dimension to the music however distracting and vulgar that dimension may be. Change of scale can be an act of creation. Unlike some painters Rosenquist does not see pictures in the fire: he looks at reality and sees abstraction. This abstraction is often a parody of slick commercial-art studio presentations, which makes his paintings both informative and funny. In her excellent introduction to a Rosenquist New York exhibition Marcia Tucker says we must 'alternate constantly between scanning and focusing as we look at a painting in order to choose whether to see an image as figure or ground'. This applies of course to one of Rosenquist's best-known early paintings, *Silver Skies*, in which a medley of Pop images – tyre, coke-bottle, pin-up and so on – need to be scanned and focused; it also applies in a more decoratively analytical sense to Roy Lichtenstein's more-than-diagrammatic *Tire*, the title of which is self-explanatory.

To a casual eye fifteen years ago this work might have seemed a mere inflection of a commercial-art catalogue drawing, but now we see it as a race between elegance and vulgarity in which the former finishes lengths ahead and where many Op art elements are present to keep the eyes in motion. The tread pattern is at one moment an irregular zigzag, then a ceremonial stairway, next an escalator. Buttresses at tread and sidewall are no doubt there for strength and to combat aquaplaning but they also lead the eye to the wheel centre and, suddenly transformed into gear-teeth, break up what might well be a banal ellipse. The sheer size no doubt was considered shocking: no mere quarter-page catalogue drawing but an oil painting on canvas measuring 68 inches by 56.

Roy Lichtenstein's 68 by 80 inch leer

named *In the Car* was the quintessence of contemporary Pop: a comic strip that is not a comic strip for the good reason that the action has been halted. There is no legend, no picture next door, but a long built-in pause, induced by the size of the image and the flat areas of colour, which focus our attention however reluctantly upon the aloofness of the blonde and the wolfishness of her escort. By inflating comic strip cartoons until the half-tone dots are half an inch wide, Lichtenstein makes us look again at what would normally be thrown away. Lichtenstein's strips, like Cézanne's apples, change our thinking. Andy Warhol, painting one hundred Campbell's soup cans, identical objects each slightly differently rendered, as if they were so many daisies, was laughing at mass production and our acceptance of the banal. With his car crash series of prints he pointed the lesson that horrors when repeated lose their power to shock: a video newsreel on the TV that recurs every hour on the hour, and loses all interest or impact.

Soon artists were to re-discover the excitement of roads, the glitter of paint, the glamour of multi-carburetters, but for the moment Pop Artists were sunk in drab urban gloom. There is more to cars, they said, than sport and enjoyment, the happy hedonism of Picabia and his white Mercedes, the great Roman-nosed Renaults of the 1920s or a Boxer Ferrari. For every sports car in the world there are ten million humdrum hacks, each the means of providing personal mobility. Some small part of the time these cars may fulfil their owners' dreams, opening up the countryside, seeking the sun, acting out the cliché known as 'Getting away from it all'; but most of the average car's mileage is a trivial round of home-to-office, ferrying children, going down to the shops. So far from getting away from it all most cars carry it all with them, an encapsulation of the subur-

bia they generate wherever they go. Instead of freedom and fresh air it is traffic jams and exhaust fumes, each set of occupants cocooned in its own frustration, sealed off from their fellow men by unopened windows, confined, like Jean Dubuffet's graffiti manikins. Parked vehicles clog the view, lights wink, sirens blare. Used-car lots overflow the sidewalk. Showrooms add a touch of opulence: status symbols on display. Beyond the city centre are the wreckers' yards. Unlikely material for art, but this is the world which Pop artists discovered in the 1950s and Photo Realists like John Salt in the 1970s.

Dead cars are a feature of the landscape in every industrial country, a natural end-product of planned obsolescence. Pressed steel has become as common as dirt, so to say, and far more available in American cities than common clay. It is a natural source of raw material for the artist. The man who in America identified himself with automotive detritus was John Chamberlain, born in Rochester, Indiana, in 1927, and he was working before the big Pop exhibitions of 1962. His well-known scrap-metal *Wildroot* of 1959 stood five feet high and was called by the critic Laurence Alloway 'junk art', although it was no different philosophically than the Abstract Expressionist paintings then at the height of fashion. It is a three-dimensional abstract built from coloured car fragments, the formal ambiguities of which liberate the fancy in the same way as the pigment in a Pollock or the square-foot of river bank from which Graham Sutherland sometimes constructs a landscape. Later Chamberlains such as *Fantail Sculpture* (1961), *Velvet White* (1962) and *Dolores James* proved more formal and cohesive, more brilliant in colour and no more related to cars save in the source of material. Chamberlain later turned to other forms of scrap, soft as well as metallic, for his constructions.

In Paris at this time another sculptor, César, had become necrophilously involved at the breakers'. Enthralled at the way the giant new press at the Société Française de la Ferraille at Gennevilliers could transform an old car into a symmetrical bale of metal in one operation, like the crusher used so dramatically to dispose of a body in the James Bond film *Goldfinger*, César determined to apply the technique artistically, the machine serving as hammer and chisel. At first, he says, he employed the medium coarsely: 'The press went beyond my intentions. Then my excitement became tempered by artistic judgement, and I tried to control the effect, to make the sort of package I wanted, from selected materials'. He told the men to put in 'bumpers only, or mudguards or bonnets. Now a black car, two red bonnets, a dozen bumper bars'. If César's relish for his medium seems tinged with *Schadenfreude*, we must accept that his complex textures and surfaces could be obtained in no other way. César moreover had other shots in his locker to which we shall return towards the end of this chapter.

César's use of selection – 'red cars, bumpers only' – is a reminder that painters too were finding inspiration in car components divorced from the parent vehicle. There is an elegant *Buick Painting* by Larry Rivers, one of the younger New York Action Painters which Hervé Poulain places on the hingeline between down-to-earth Pop (*art de constat*) and lyrical abstraction, in which the wings and toothily grinning grille become softened by broad brushwork so that one thinks not only of Rauschenberg but of Nicholas de Staël. One thinks also of *Sunbeam Tiger* by the English painter and sculptor Anthony Twentyman, in which an abstract painting was inspired by the exciting shapes and inspired technicalities of a famous racing engine. Both paintings date from the early 1960s, and one should perhaps remember that at that time, Surrealist paintings in the manner of the 1930s were still being done. It was in 1960 that René Magritte painted a jockey galloping lightly across the roof of a bourgeois limousine. This, apart from a taxi by Dali and the same artist's brickwork saloon in *The Town of Delft*, is one of the few Surrealist paintings on a motoring theme. Is there somewhere a Paul Delvaux containing a car? Surely somewhere behind the classical columns in that unearthly dreamscape through which his naked ladies glide there must be parked a coupé de ville?

The idea would have appealed to Isidore Ducasse, 'Comte de Lautréamont', whose *Les Chants de Maldoror* a hundred years before had contained the phrase, adopted as a text by the Surrealists, 'as beautiful as the chance meeting on a dissecting table of a sewing-machine and an umbrella'. In 1868 a sewing-machine was the last word in progress, the equivalent of a space-capsule or hologram today; and it was similar chance meetings of incongruous or poetically related objects which Richard Hamilton and Peter Phillips delighted to exploit in their Pop compositions – for want of a better term – of the 1960s. In a Phillips the perspectives and changes in

depth make our eyes click like, as someone remarked, 'very expensive marble tiles on a lavatory floor'. Hard-edge rainbows; Chinese-box-like structures somehow suggesting ball-races; an American eagle; a radiator grille; urgently upstanding lipsticks; a catalogue drawing of a sectioned transmission; realistic girlie nudes – all these images linger in the mind. They float in his compositions at different depths and may with practice be read in 3-D as an engineer reads a blueprint. These paintings are tough, technological, two-pence-coloured and erotic. Which will do as a description of Pop art until a better one comes along. Do they qualify as car paintings? Perhaps not; but then nor does Rauschenberg's *Dylaby*, which is not a painting at all but an example of junk recycled to make a poetic statement: a decaying tyre transfixed by an old door daubed with a two-way arrow. An ambiguous end of the road, with overtones of witchcraft – the stake through the heart.

Hardly less of a stake through the soft heart of America was the 'Tin Lizzie' Ford dyptich of Robert Indiana, otherwise Robert Clark, who adopted the name of his native state. Like Tom Wesselmann in his series of Monroe-based 'Great American Nudes' Indiana is here tilting at everything the media held sacred, in brilliant colour and literal realism that anyone could understand. He is not only pointing the same moral, or immoral, as Lichtenstein's *In the Car*, but sniping at the great American folk memory and playing irreverent generation games with the Matriarchy, most sacred of national institutions. The smart stencilled lettering 'A MOTHER IS A MOTHER' recalls Gertrude Stein's 'a rose is a rose is a rose', and the 1927 registration plate of the Model T sedan by which the parents stand, so respectable, demure and unbuttoned, need not be irrelevant. Indiana delights in folk and literary allusions especially when barbed, and he would have known John Steinbeck's remark in *Cannery Row*: 'Someone should write an erudite essay on the moral, physical and esthetic effect of the Model T Ford on the American nation. Two generations of Americans knew more about the Ford coil than the clitoris, about the planetary system of gears than the solar system of the stars. . . . Most of the babies of the period were conceived in Model T Fords and not a few were born in them'.

In spirit if not in style one is reminded of the aimless, sometimes naked, journeyings in Jack Kerouac's 'beat' novel *On the Road* (1959) that had so coloured American thinking some seven years before,

In A Father is a Father *and* A Mother is a Mother *Robert Indiana shows the characteristic irreverence of Pop Art towards accepted American standards. Here he is tilting at the Model T, fount of American mythology, and even at Matriarchy itself.*

Right: *Peter Phillips's* Automobilia *(1972–3) assembles car elements in an intricate juxtaposition of synthetic, machine-made colours and textures which, thanks to the superimposed strips, appeared to be floating in space.*

although the artist who comes inescapably to mind in the latter connexion is Ed Kienholz, whose assemblage *Back Seat Dodge* must be one of the nastiest as well the most compelling of all three-dimensional car-pieces. Taking his raw material from a breaker's yard Kienholz has 'cut and shut' an old car so that the front wings and bonnet adjoin the back seat: a vehicle symbolizing human life, nasty, brutish and short. Amongst the mixed media some underwear caught in the windscreen; in the back human detritus simulated from chicken wire and stockings. A brilliant, fossilized grope.

A very different, more optimistic and traditional view is held by Allan d'Arcangelo, who is fascinated by the road itself; not the tree-lined roads and racing circuits of the old world but the American highway, shortest distance between two diners. D'Arcangelo began combining techniques of hard-edge painting, already familiar through the work of Frank Stella, with a lyrical geometry he made very much his own. Working in acrylic on large canvases he gives us white lines slicing away into the distance, visible for miles although dimly lit, with the clear colour and flat surfaces characteristic of the medium; roads unrelieved by buildings although diversified here and there by a tree, advertisement or the driver's own rear-view mirror. Beyond the hill must lie an equally hard-edge geometrical and hygienic new *Standard* service station by Edward Ruscha, brashly lit against a night

sky. U.S. painting of this period incidentally is not easy for the ordinary household to collect, for Allan D'Arcangelo's *Highway No. 2* measures 6 ft by 6 ft 9 in, while Ruscha's canvas of the roadside filling station is 5 ft 5 in by just over 10 feet.

Commercial art techniques had already been borrowed, exploited, adapted and ridiculed during the Pop Art explosion as part of the revolt against Abstract Expressionism. After years when paint and paint alone had counted, young artists had turned to real life at one remove, aiming a shrewd and painful kick at the media through which America absorbed its observations and attitudes. The joke, however, was fairly short lived. Existentialism is not an abiding philosophy. Commercial art, though, still had a considerable mileage. The vast billboard images which James Rosenquist and his colleagues spread across the cities were accepted by the mass as reality.

Meanwhile a new instrument of perception had come into people's hands. This was the eye-level single-lens reflex camera. By the early 1960s cheapish Japanese SLR (single-lens reflex) cameras were available in the United States, each with a variety of interchangeable lenses, from wide-angle to telephoto for long-range close-ups. For an artist this was a wonderful tool, an adjustable window on the world through which subjects could be seen from any angle and at almost any magnification, blurred or razor-sharp; and not only seen but captured 'as viewed' in

monochrome or colour. But there was a difference. A camera does not, cannot, see things in the same way as the human eye: the camera glimpses, the eye is in constant motion, scanning the subject patch by tiny patch. A camera lens working at a small aperture renders everything in sharp focus and thus provides a view that the human eye has never seen but which artists at various times have been at pains to attempt. Vermeer and Pieter de Hoogh, by showing everything sharply, from, for example, a broom in the foreground to a street seen through a long passageway (in Pieter de Hoogh's *Courtyard in Delft* in the National Gallery, London). This is what Edward Weston, the brilliant American photographer of the 1920s, educated his camera to do by working with very small

apertures ('the f/64 Club'). The 17th-century Dutchmen's concern with painting everything sharply and in its own texture has remained Everyman's conception of reality ever since, only faintly dented by the Impressionists' heretical views on coloured shadows, and the way in which structures are changed by the way light falls upon them.

An unlikely experimenter with photographic realism in its latterday form was Tom Wesselmann, one of the Pop Art originators from the Sydney Janis Gallery, New York, in 1962. Two years later, interrupting his stylized, streamlined, infinitely beguiling series of the Great American Nude somewhere about number 70, Wesselmann focused his attention on another mid-century symbol, the Volkswagen

Above: *Robert Bechtle, who painted this 62 Chevy when the car was nostalgically nine years old, is easier to read than some of the Photo Realist school, but his 'realism' is deceptive nonetheless. The subject here is in fact distorted as though taken through a wide-angle lens and the car appears artificially primped up, like the models in a girlie magazine.*

Right: *Ralph Goings paints as meticulously as a 17th-century Dutch master, although his subjects are very much of our time. He aims to render textures and reflections with complete fidelity. This for him is the challenge.* Sherwin William's Chevy *dates from 1975. Below:* John Salt's *Two Chevies in Wreck Yard, although Photo Realist, is most complex if viewed from a photographic standpoint: a wide-angle close-up with great depth of field, but with the foreground cars slightly out of focus while those behind are in focus. It is a classic demonstration that Photo Realist painting is not always what it seems.*

Beetle, presenting the car head-on in catalogue detail but slightly blurred, as a sort of collage against a spoof travel poster. This was Pop-anecdotal; but like James Rosenquist in *Broome Street Truck* which dates from the same period, Wesselmann is exploring the play of reflections and shadows on a curved surface. In 1966 Rosenquist went one better on this idea in his *Car Touch*, a pair of 9-foot canvases motorized so that they collide with one another, bumper to chromium bumper, an extension of the shiny-panel paintings which were made some three years before.

From such experiments emerged a new form of realism which was to shock the abstract traditionalist, horrify the art schools and cause more young artists to paint car subjects than ever before. In 1971 a New York dealer, Ivan Karp, gave a lecture (I quote from Linda Chase, *Photo Realism*, Eminent Publications, New York, 1975) 'to a gathering of realist painters at the Alliance for Social Progress on East Broadway. The dominance of first abstract, then Pop, Minimal, and Conceptual art since the 1950s had created difficulties for representational artists, and one might have expected them to welcome this new form of realism, which was already pumping new lifeblood into their cause and might even open some of the doors modernism had slammed in their faces'. Instead, slides of Ralph Goings's pick-up trucks, Richard McLean's horses, Robert Bechtle's suburban cars and Richard Estes's chrome and glass buildings were met with cries of 'Obscene!' and 'Pornography!' The audience's outrage was clear and shocking.

Every new art movement creates indignation. The studio realists cried 'Obscene!' and 'Pornographic!' no doubt precisely because the new painters had stripped their favourite subjects of the subjective approach and decent abstraction in which they had been shrouded for so long. One wonders what they would have thought of Carl de Andrea's life-size polychrome Photo Realist figures. De Andrea's figures

Left: *Don Eddy is immensely accomplished at painting reflections, as witness this work* Untitled *(1971). Here again we have a view of a Volkswagen 'Beetle' that could only be caught by a painter – it would not be apparent to the naked eye, or to a camera lens.*

are 'real' and yet they are unnaturally still; and the same can be said of most Photo Realist cars. They sit for their portraits. Their engines do not run and it matters not at all what make or type they may be. The 'lazy afternoon' look in a Robert Bechtle painting like *Chrysler, T. Bird* is deliberate. He avoids motion which, he says, 'makes sense in a photograph but which becomes false in a painting because painting is essentially a static art'.

The Photo Realists are mostly young men, who combine a feeling for paint with a very strong feeling for photography. There must be as many approaches as there are artists. Richard Estes tries in his paintings to capture the quality of a colour transparency, and this is no mean task on an oil painting measuring perhaps 5 feet by 6, when the original is a 35-mm slide. Too small to be looked at directly, it loses its luminosity when projected, and if printed it goes flat. 'It loses something: surface'. A camera provides the basis but the painter remains in control. One thinks of Mrs. Julia Margaret Cameron, the greatest of early photographers and regarded as a heretic by the Establishment: 'When focusing and coming to something which to my eye was very beautiful I stopped there instead of screwing on the lens to the more definite focus that all other photographers insist on'. Photo Realist paintings seem to have been built up from a number of exposures focused on separate points in the composition, and sometimes one suspects that these have been taken with lenses of varying focal length. Richard Estes has written that he may eliminate features he does not want or move things about, 'make this line a little stronger, things like that' – as a landscape painter may adjust the position of a barn or eliminate a telephone pole. But Richard Estes is very much an urban creature. From early paintings of shop fronts he moved on to cars. They were part of the raw city in which he was brought up. He is also on record as saying he does not enjoy looking at the things he paints and he does not see why we should enjoy it either. He simply enjoys the challenge posed by putting them on canvas.

John Salt, the expatriate Englishman born in Birmingham in 1937 comes closer to Mrs. Cameron's soft-focus technique than the other Photo Realists. He enjoys soft surfaces, perhaps even an artistic *flou*. The upholstery in his derelict cars looks somehow sinister – like the lining of a coffin, Maître Hervé Poulain has suggested, soft and fat. This softness applies not only to the interior trim of the cars he finds lying about but to the cellulose too, which has a deathly hush, probably because he paints in a non-traditional way with spray gun and air brush. In his work one finds the multi-focus approach, possibly unconscious, and an effect that no camera lens would be likely to produce. In a

129

In Wrecking Yard III *Don Eddy is concerned not only with the play of light on paintwork and chromium but with portraying objects in depth: he focuses on the wire fence and leaves the wreck to speak for itself.*

painting called *Pioneer Pontiac* (1972–1973) the view is from immediately behind a battered wreck; tin cans and grass in the foreground are sharp; so are the whole of the car's flank and an advertisement on the corrugated iron shed behind, but bushes against which the car stands seem more painterly than photographic. Salt is quoted as saying that 'the photograph wiped out art history for you; it let you see reality before art history was invented'. Oddly enough, though, it reminds me of the early photographers, who worked with small stops, uncorrected lenses and coarse printing paper. The work of the American Bill Colin, too, has painterly qualities that the pioneer photographers strove to bring off. Colin's *37 Packard* in its

nest of grass and setting of worm-eaten shed is a large painting 51 inches by 76 painted in acrylic on canvas, but it reminds us irresistibly of a Calotype study by Fox Talbot or Adamson and Hill in the 1840s taken on paper negative and printed on textured rag paper – a case of art illustrating the history of photography.

Just as the Early Victorian 'dark box' gave artists a new way of looking at things whether they liked it or not, so the modern single-lens reflex with its interchangeable objectives has provided a new kind of 'reality'. Close-ups are no longer a problem, thanks to wide-angle, and it is well known to television viewers that racing cars ride in closely-packed bunches thanks to the wonders of 'zoom'. When every tourist is

armed with an SLR and artists use them as a tool of the trade there has of course been a realist revival. It would be naive to see this as a return to Victorian genre painting, in which artists pitted their descriptive skill against flowers, dead game, fish and the bloom on grapes. The new realists look elsewhere for subjects and work on a far larger scale. Yet Ralph Goings (born Corning, California, 1928) became interested in Jeeps, pick-ups and caravans for the same reason that Landseer painted dead birds. Like Landseer, he desired to paint still-lifes, but he added another dimension, that of the photograph. He wishes to paint what is there, but like a good photographer he is concerned with the quality of the shadows and highlights as well as their distribu-

tion. He is very conscious, he says, of not making any kind of judgement or comment about the subject matter other than that 'It's a terribly beautiful thing to paint'. Here we have the nub of the matter, the revolution of the past twenty years: rendering instead of abstraction has become the major preoccupation. Formality has returned. Just as the Impressionists abandoned the imagined ideal landscape in favour of impressions collected over a period of minutes so Photo Realists now isolate the impression of say 1/500 of a second. Ralph Goings is illuminating on this. He is not interested in a brief subjective impression, nor yet in an idealization, a catalogue illustrator's ideal of a caravan:

'Maybe the paintings would be a little more naturalistic, in the sense of kind of trashy and rough and coarse, if they were done over a period of two or three days . . .' But his are done over a period of forty-five to fifty days, and one day's work – one eight or ten-hour day's work – may be devoted to three or four square inches of canvas. The collector who buys a Ralph Goings buys a very careful distillation indeed, by no means a 5 by 7 foot blow-up of a colour slide of a caravan.

Don Eddy (born Long Beach, California 1944) is the master of reflections, interested in formal visual problems. Stand beside him and you will be looking at, for example, cars in a show-room with the various reflections and colours picked up by their paintwork and chrome. But there are phantasmal car reflections on the glass through which you are looking, and also, you become aware, on the glass at right angles to it, through which you can see cars parked in a side street, and buildings

131

Andrew Holmes, English architect, is interested especially in American cars as a Photo Realist subject. Astonishingly, this 1957 Cadillac 60-S in wide-angle was not painted in acrylic but drawn on cartridge paper with Derwent coloured pencils.

Brendan Neiland, born at Lichfield, Staffordshire in 1941, is interested in reflections in cars and buildings; he trained at the Birmingham College of Art and the Royal College. His larger works are all in acrylic on canvas; this one, Reflector, is a screenprint.

across the way, as well as reflections of those buildings in the window and lettering on the window-glass itself. This is all very formal, and sharp, but although apparently photographic it is no photo that ever was or could be: it is a synthesis which may be compared with a painted portrait, evolved not by one glimpse but over a number of sittings.

In an interview with Nancy Foote (in *Art in America*, Nov./Dec. 1972) Eddy explained that his paintings are not simply photographic: 'A camera makes only two distinctions: one is focus and the other is value. Neither of these qualities in my paintings is photographic because I take

several photographs and then work from the one which gives me the kind of information I need for that area. I do my own developing and printing, and I can print to bring out different value scales. I also take a number of photographs that give me different focal points.' Two analogies suggest themselves here. We think of the blueprints which, given a plan, an elevation and a cross-section enable an engineer to visualize a piece 'in the round'; and one recalls the Picasso portraits of his middle period in which interlocking profiles and elements from other viewpoints were used to build up an often startling likeness. Eddy and Estes among the Photo Realists often combine information in their paintings which has been culled from several viewpoints, and in this they have a direct link with the Cubist, Vorticist and Futurist movements.

Amongst the Photo Realists Stateside, motor sport was by no means forgotten, although it was portrayed 'at the halt'. Robert Cottingham specialized originally in paintings of American cinema architecture, making play with the neon-tubes, lettering and shadows in the original Photo Realist manner. More recently he has shown a penchant for racing engines, like his fellow artists Tom Blackwell and Chris Cross. The early work of another American, Ron Kleeman, combined f/64 depth of field with glossy reflectionist highlights (e.g. *Leo's Revenge*, 1971) and Surreal anecdotal surroundings; his *Skidoo 23* (1973) lovingly depicts the glitter and gloss of a racing stock car, and is painted, so to say, with a wide-angle lens and extremely small stop. Everything is pin-sharp from radiator to windscreen, and every sparkle in place. Kleeman homes in equally lovingly on racing engines and fire trucks. It is strange how chromium has replaced smoke, gravel and 'pork' as a symbol of speed.

Although the subjects and cars in Andrew Holmes's work are American the artist himself is English. Born in 1947 he trained at the Architectural Association in London and while there made many drawings which included both buildings and cars. Like the American Photo Realist painters he is interested largely in the shapes into which car panelling has been formed, in the glossy texture of the paintwork and the reflections from plated bright-work.

Ben Johnson, an important new English talent first seen in a motoring connexion with *Glass Door Reflecting Citroën* (1973), found an impressively 'cool' way of avoiding an excess of reflections, which he rightly felt had by that time become a cliché. In 1976 Johnson produced – in monochrome as a challenge – a large painting of the Ferrari 512 which had recently broken the British landspeed record, in which the formal problems involved in looking down upon a large car from a relatively short distance produced a canvas of marked originality. Johnson works not with brush but with a spray-gun at relatively low pressure – so that it comes out in spurts – and also employs masking and resists, subsequently worked over. Also an architectural painter, he may perhaps be prevailed upon to return sometimes to cars. This Ferrari in repose somehow appears more animated than the highly glossy and exciting paintings of Californian hot-rods and racing engines by such experienced Photo Realists as Robert Cottingham, Tom Blackwell and Chris Cross.

The *sportif* who lies so closely under a Frenchman's skin has found expression in the late 1970s through the pen of François Dallegret, who has raised to the ninth degree those racing car fantasies that every schoolboy used to send to the papers. One which comes to mind is a sling-shot dragster powered by an imaginary flat-sixteen, the cycle-tyred wheels some two yards in front connected to the rest by the thinnest and most faithful of drilled side-members and steering-tubes – a lyrical little drawing in Indian ink on clear transparent plastic. An equally delightful fantasy of Dallegret's is a front view of a hyperwagnerian Vintage car drawn also in Indian ink, de-

signed to make Excalibur look like a penknife. This is collaged alongside a photographic background of Park Avenue, New York, and mounted on plywood pierced with winking lights. Two other amusements from the same artist are a pair of sketches, *Highway Zero* and *Highway Four*, both of them cloverleaf intersections leading nowhere. Other European developments of recent years are photocollages by Bertini, and the experiments of Massimo Rotella, who has produced images of considerable power and complexity by means of photographic screenprints, superimposing one shot upon another (as in his car interior entitled *Bonjour*) with and without a texturing of dots from a half-tone block. Rotella has exploited the pictorial possibilities of peeling posters on billboards in a *décollage* based on a Monza motor racing poster of 1963.

Ben Johnson (b.1946) is another English artist with strong architectural leanings. He is also concerned with light and textures. This most interesting black and white acrylic painting (1976) provides a bird's eye view of the rebuilt Ferrari 512 M in which Robert Horne set a British Speed Record of nearly 200 mph. The open 'gull-wing' doors add to the interest of the composition.

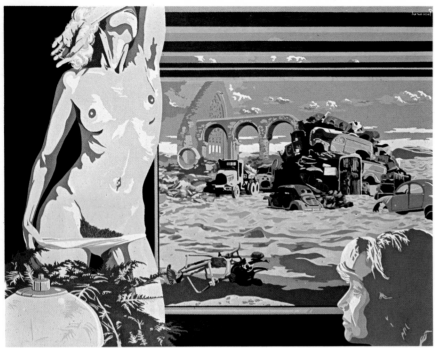

Top left: This powerful memento mori is by the French painter Pascarel, who calls it L'Expression de mes meilleurs sentiments *(1973).*
Above: L'Hommage à Monsieur Ingres *by Mario Avati must be almost the only motoring mezzotint. The nude at the window is taken from a French commemorative stamp. Also commemorative is the astonishing César (top right) in which the sculptor has compressed some 40 motor racing cups won over the years by the French driver and art collector Hervé Poulain.*

Decaying posters far more than brash new ones add interest and diversity to urban sites and oddly few artists have turned them to account; they would be rewarding in gouache, Photo Realism, or indeed that most textural of all media, mezzotint, but the only motoring mezzotint that comes to mind is Mario Avati's *L'Hommage à Monsieur Ingres.* This is outwardly an evocation of an Edwardian 'doctor's coupé', only the highlights showing against the velvet blackness; but in the passenger's window, brilliant as though floodlit and crossed as by the bars of a Venetian blind, is a classical nude by Ingres. At first sight a framed painting, the latter is in fact a French 1 franc postage stamp magnified several times.

César (born César Baldaccini), has, as already noted, another shot in his locker besides the famous *compressions.* Since about 1970 he has experimented with expansions as well. The technique is to pour polyurethane and its appropriate hardener and direct the flow into sculptural patterns. The 'accidental' results of César's technique provoked the same kind of hostility as the misunderstood technique of Action Painting. Since then César has applied his solidified foam in other directions; and since he has motor-racing friends he has impressed his wit on discarded cylinder-blocks and doors. This resurrection conferred by César makes a welcome antidote to the modern Surrealist pessimism of Charles Pascarel, for example (*L'Expression de mes meilleurs sentiments,* 1973), and to the horrifying abstracts of the Czechoslovakian painter Franta, whose abstracts of motor accident scenes put Warhol into reverse. They have the compelling horror of a realistic Crucifixion, or of Fox's *Book of Martyrs.*

But away with gloom. The world's foremost collector of motoring art, Maître Hervé Poulain, to whom the author of this book owes more than he can ever repay, is also a racing driver. After a successful career in sprints, hillclimbs and short races he entered for the 24 Hours of Le Mans in 1975, with a 3.5-litre B.M.W. What more natural – and more brilliant – than to approach Alexander Calder, then living in France, as the *fons et origo* of 'Mobiles' to create him a road-going 'mobile' in the form of a B.M.W. racing car for Le Mans. A model was made and was decorated by Alexander Calder; it is shown against a background of Calder mobiles. Subsequent motor cars in the Hervé Poulain équipes have been painted by Roy Lichtenstein and Frank Stella. The 1978 car was by Andy Warhol.

In addition, Hervé Poulain possesses perhaps the most exciting César of all: a compression of some forty or so cups and trophies that he has won during his racing career. It is a lyrical solution to the problem of sideboard silverware, infinitely more decorative and compelling than the silver table-top which the Auto Union driver Hans Stuck had cast from his own collection of trophies.

One can but agree with the friend who told Poulain, 'You have made your mark as a driver, but César has brought you fame.'

Art in Action

Above: *Alexander Calder the American sculptor (b.1898) invented the 'mobile'; he also lived in France, at Gache. What was more natural than for the art collector Hervé Poulain when driving at Le Mans for the first time, (with the American, Sam Posey) to ask Calder to decorate his highly mobile 3.5 litre B.M.W? A model was made which Calder decorated. Here this model and the 1975 Le Mans car are seen against a background of Calder mobiles at Gache. Unfortunately the 'mobile' motor stopped at 8 pm while lying first in its class and fifth overall. Far left: a front view of the Calder car. Lower picture, far left: Frank Stella's 3.5 litre 1976 B.M.W.; in contrast to Calder's exuberant 1975 decoration, Stella's is cool, measured, set down on engineers' drawing paper. Near left: The 1977 car as painted by Roy Lichenstein, in the pits at Le Mans. The half-tone dots and yellow stripes suggest a tiger or leopard.*

Something for Every Taste

Sculpture, mascots and objets d'art

Above: *Incongruously united with a classical goddess upon the pediment above the main entrance to the Argyll company's grandiose factory at Alexandria near Dumbarton stands this sculptured car. But is it from the same hand?* Facing page: *Hispano-Suiza aero-engines were used in the Spad fighters flown by the Escadrille des Cigognes, whose badge was a stork, so when car production was resumed after World War I, the company chose a stork as their mascot.*

FROM TOULOUSE-LAUTREC and Robida's *La fin du cheval* to César and the Photo Realists stretch eight decades of motoring art. So far from there being a dearth of material, as seemed likely when this study began, an almost embarrassing quantity has come to light, representing every school from pompier to Hyper Realism by way of Dada and race-reporting. Almost every artists' material used for drawing or painting is represented, and cars have been captured in every mood. Today, when naturalism is once more respectable and abstraction is in retreat, motor cars are at last accepted as fit subjects for a gallery painting, although this is no palace revolution brought about from within through the efforts of motoring painters, but a movement independent of the automobile as such. Unlike Montaut, Crosby and Ham, who looked for movement, drama and sport, the American Photo Realists see automobiles as a painterly problem. They paint cars not for what they are or could be, but simply because they are there. The very difficulty of the subject, which once frightened away all but the specialist artist, now attracts talent from outside the circle. We have the brilliant showroom paintings of Don Eddy and Richard Estes, the external and under-bonnet close-ups of Ron Kleeman and the 'still-life with manifold' which Tom Blackwell calls *Triple Carburettor 'GTO'*. The latter at least should delight Ferrari-

fanciers as much as does Ben Johnson's elegant 512M.

Collectors of 'automobiliana' have plenty of choice. Some specialize in posters, for which there has been too little room in these pages: one would like to have included examples by PAL (Paléologue) by Sévelinge and by Grasset from the Belle Epoque, Misty of mid-Edwardian days, some more Cassandre, and, moving down the French time-scale, P. Beligond, G. Leygnac and Savignac of the 1960s and 1970s. There are transatlantic names too: Edward Penfield, Coles Philips, Layendecker, Louis Fancher, and artists from Britain including John Hassall (1868–1948), Edward McKnight Kauffer (1890–1954), F. C. Harrison, P. C. Kelly and Ashley Havinden (1903–1973).

Some public sculpture has already been mentioned, notably the Levassor and Serpollet monuments in Paris, but visitors to Loch Lomond should spare a glance for the pediment above the entrance to the old Argyll car factory at Alexandria near Glasgow, because it frames a stone carving of an Edwardian motor car, no less. If the tourist then heads south, pausing at Derby, he may see a full-length statue of Sir Henry Royce by F. Derwent Wood, R.A., and then proceed to Dover for a contemporary view of that great man's partner, the Honourable C. S. Rolls by Lady Scott, gazing out to sea as perhaps he did when planning his two-

way flight across the Channel in 1910. Motor racing enthusiasts already have two excellent reasons for going to Donington Park, near Leicester, the circuit and the Wheatcroft Collection of single-seaters, but in the Paddock they will find a third, namely the bronze portrait plaque modelled by 'B. Bira' in memory of his friend and fellow E.R.A. driver Pat Fairfield, who crashed at Le Mans in 1937. Under his real name, H. H. Prince Birabongse of Thailand, Bira studied sculpture under Sir Charles Wheeler, P.R.A.

Small motoring bronzes are nothing like so plentiful as *animalier* works, although racing cars were a fairly popular theme during the Heroic Age. Many of them are unsigned (and often cast in spelter rather than bronze) but one should look out for casts showing Baron Pierre de Caters's Mercedes of about 1905, which sometimes carries a clock in the nose of its cowled radiator; this is slightly later than the Moreau-Vauthier bronze Mors discussed on page 25, and the china box on the same theme which the sculptor made with the help of the ceramist Decoeur. All these were included in the now dispersed collection of James O. Barron, together with a silver-plated bronze standish in the form of an Alfonso XIII model Hispano-Suiza of

about 1913, an attractive ornament for any enthusiast's desk, with its places for inkwells and pens. The French continued this fondness for decorative bronze car models throughout the great years of 1920 to 1930, although these were often examples of model-making rather than works of art. The same goes for the desirable silver creations of such London silversmiths as Asprey, Garrard's, and Mappin & Webb. Wealthy owners used often to commemorate their cars and yachts in this way, and silver models were sometimes made to celebrate achievements. An especially charming presentation group was made after the heroic crossing of the Sahara by a party of 7 hp Jowetts in the 1920s. Complete with cars and palm trees this was a 'primitive', not simply a model.

In France bronzes and motoring sculpture have been enjoying a revival. César has continued his investigations into crushability. By varying the diet fed to his hydraulic press he produces a range of shapes and textures unobtainable by other means, polychrome sculptural masses which have grown in respectability over the years, psychologically as well as aesthetically interesting because they appeal to both the creative and destructive instincts. The constructions of Loïc

Racing cars were a popular subject for ornaments during the Heroic Age; they also decorated objects like this pen-tray.

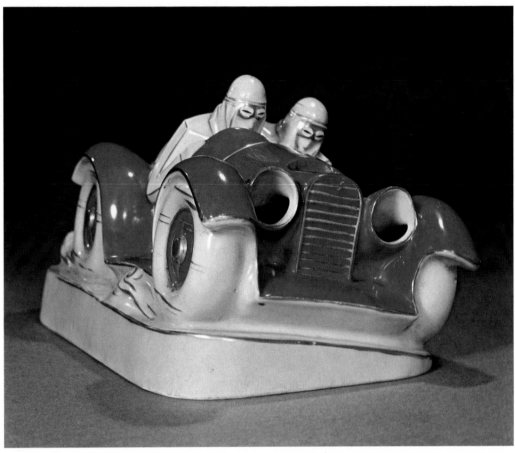

Dubigeon cover some of the same ground since they depict modern Formula I racing cars as they appear all too often in real life – bent after leaving the road. Despite their obvious immobility these wounded machines appear far more real than a photograph, scale model or film because they have weight, and presence, and also the emotional content which distinguishes a good portrait.

A similar intensity emanates from the sculpture of that other Frenchman, Olivier Brice. Brice exploits the mystery and ambiguities which drapery confers. Draped figures have been common in sculpture since the earliest times, and sheeted cars are a feature of every motor show on press day, but Olivier Brice must be the first to drape cars as an artist drapes his model. Familiar shapes become interesting when partly concealed, a principle demonstrated by ladies of the Directoire in their clinging chiffon gowns, and by any girl who discovers the seductive properties of a veil. But Olivier Brice has also a sombre side. Sometimes the veil becomes a shroud, the draperies a winding-sheet: there could be no more moving monument to a racing driver than the draped Tyrrell by which Brice remembers the popular Formula I driver François Cevert.

The most frequent form of motoring sculpture of course was the mascot for mounting on radiator-cap, scuttle or roof. The majority of those produced had no artistic merit, comprising for the most part crudely modelled female figures, horses' heads and fox-terriers sold cheaply by the accessory manufacturers. Rather better as a rule were mascots associated with the make of car, like the Hispano stork recalling the use of Hispano-Suiza aero-engines by Guynmer's SPAD escadrille on the Western Front, and the Rolls-Royce Spirit

Nothing could be more Art Deco than this little French car (above, left) in the French racing colour, blue, heightened with gilt. Somewhere, remaining to be discovered there must be a male companion to this Edwardian motoring lady in porcelain (above, right), made at the Amphora pottery at Teplitz in Austria. Below: a most moving memorial to a racing driver: the Tyrell of François Cevert in its shroud, by the French sculptor, Olivier Brice.

The Rolls-Royce Lady

Perhaps the most famous mascot of all: Spirit of Ecstacy. *This drawing of the 'Rolls-Royce lady' is by the sculptor of the original, Charles Sykes, R.A. The statue to the Hon. C. S. Rolls regarding the scene of his double Channel crossing is by Lady Scott.*

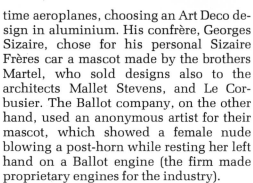

The Sphinx has always been popular as a mascot subject. Those shown are from an Armstrong Siddeley Sapphire and a Black Hawk Stutz. Below: Very rare is this meerschaum pipe in the Geoffroi de Beauffort collection. Only one other example is known.

of Ecstasy modelled by Charles Sykes (1875–1950) for the 40–50 hp Rolls-Royce as a standing figure and afterwards repeated on a smaller scale in a kneeling position. The stately Minerva car, Belgian rival to Rolls-Royce, carried a head of the goddess Minerva modelled by the well-known Belgian sculptor Pierre de Soete (1886–1948), and the Vulcan car made in Southport, Lancashire, had a standing figure of Vulcan, the smith of the gods. Similarly Rover carried a Viking sea-rover. The stylized head of another mythical figure, the Sphinx, formed the mascot of America's most successful sports car, the vertical-eight Stutz. Gabriel Voisin, maker of the Avions Voisin car, used a wing motif to remind people of his pioneering and war-

time aeroplanes, choosing an Art Deco design in aluminium. His confrère, Georges Sizaire, chose for his personal Sizaire Frères car a mascot made by the brothers Martel, who sold designs also to the architects Mallet Stevens, and Le Corbusier. The Ballot company, on the other hand, used an anonymous artist for their mascot, which showed a female nude blowing a post-horn while resting her left hand on a Ballot engine (the firm made proprietary engines for the industry).

In England there was a vogue during the 1920s for humorous mascots created by well-known cartoonists. John Hassall did several, including an airman with adjustable head and revolving propeller, and a comic policeman. George Studdy, the humorous artist responsible for the comic bull-terrier pup, 'Bonzo', naturally offered Bonzo car mascots, and many cars carried effigies of Bruce Bairnsfather's archetypal British soldier 'Old Bill' from the Great War, complete with tin hat and walrus moustache.

Owners of that magnificent folly the Bugatti Royale (of whom there were only two apart from the Bugatti family) were privileged to ride behind a symbolic elephant modelled many years before by the manufacturer's sculptor brother, Rembrandt Bugatti. Contemporary with the Royale, that is to say dating from the years between the 1925 Arts Décoratifs exhibition and the Wall Street crash, were the glass mascots of René Lalique, which could be had with or without a metal

plinth concealing a light-bulb, and added a pleasantly luxurious touch to the right kind of car.

Lalique mascots inevitably come to mind when motoring glassware is discussed but they are by no means the earliest examples of decorative glass. Anonymous craftsmen were already busy by 1827 engraving large glass toddy-rummers with steam-coach scenes like the Goldsworthy Gurney goblet on page 11, using the classic method of a revolving copper wheel fed with oil and abrasive. This technique is still employed, although the author knows of no copper-wheel engraving of a motoring subject. Laurence Whistler, whose poetic concept *Exact Time* is illustrated here, works with a diamond-pointed stylus in a mixture of stipple and line engraving, while Stephen Rickard uses an adaptation of a dentist's drill. It is odd that engraved glass is not commissioned more frequently as a change from medals and cups, and odd too that Baccarat glass paperweights incorporating an automobile motif should be so rare. At the time of writing experts have discovered only a single example, which is now in the Geoffroi de Beauffort collection. Motorcar pictures in stained glass are also rare, but are increasing in numbers because the only known practitioner of the art, Paul Marioni, born at Cincinnati, Ohio, in 1941, is very active in California evolving a variety of new techniques. His subjects have included a number of classic cars, including Bugatti Royale, Auburn, Cadillac and

Dodge, together with subjects from the Heroic Age of motoring.

In the days when horseless carriages were considered unmentionable except in allegorical or mythological terms, the establishment hung back, but there was great activity amongst less hidebound artists and craftsmen, who produced a bewildering array of decorative wares. Automobile pictures were woven in silk (generically known as Stevengraphs), and embossed on ashtrays, pen-knives, paper-knives, buttons and menu holders. Gold and silver filigree cars were made into jewellery and ornaments. Engraved and enamelled watchcases proved very popular. There were even meerschaum tobacco-pipes made like cars, while two generations of artists were kept busy designing enamel badges for manufacturers and automobile clubs; S. C. H. Davis, for example, designed the British Racing Driver's Club car badge.

There is almost no artistic discipline, no material or technique which has not been brought to bear on motoring themes since mechanical transport began more than 120 years ago. The past ten years or so have added brilliant new names to the list of motoring artists, especially in France and the United States. Paradoxically this happened only after the motorcar had shed most of that smart, sporting, glamorous image which had for so long attracted the specialist and repelled the academician. It was left to specialists like Montaut, Crosby and Geo Ham to find ways of rendering speed, report the races, chronicle changes

Motor cars may seem an anachronistic subject for a stained-glass window, but the craft is in fact highly flourishing, especially in California. A leading stained-glass artist is Paul Marioni, whose version of Ernest Montaut's Un Match Moderne *appears on page 33. The large picture shows his* Bugatti Royale *(using an actual headlamp lens); the* lower one is of a couple in their Delage is entitled 25 Years.

in car design and keep the enthusiasts happy. With the exception of Ernest Montaut who took note of every new movement, motoring illustrators were little influenced by the avant-garde; on the other hand inventive artists like Vlaminck, Derain, Bonnard and Picabia, although themselves closely involved with the pioneer and sporting phases of motoring, had no use for 'mere representation'. They and their confrères, innovators and explorers as all artists must be, were working at a time of artistic ferment, when the fruits of the Industrial Revolution were spilling into the streets. During the first half of the century art was evolving as rapidly as technology. Fauvism, Cubism, Expressionism, Futurism, Dada and the rest were paralleled by high-tension ignition, overhead camshafts, streamlining, superchargers, independent suspension. The original Fauve show in 1905 coincided with the first six-cylinder engines, *Joie de Vivre* by Matisse dead-heated with the last of the Gordon Bennett races, Picasso painted his *Demoiselles d'Avignon* just as Rolls and Royce were launching the Silver Ghost.

The list could be prolonged indefinitely. Art and engineering never stand still; and if artists, like engineers, confront us sometimes with works which are wayward, hard to master, dangerous even, these are often the most rewarding in the long run. Certainly automobile art, like motoring itself, offers something for every taste.

Index

Figures in italics refer to illustration captions

AUTOMOBILES R

 SOCIÉTÉ DES ANCIENS ÉTABL
 23, Avenue de la GRANDE ARMÉE